C000083347

Essentials of Yoruba Grammar

ESSENTIALS OF YORUBA GRAMMAR

OLADELE AWOBULUYI

UNIVERSITY PRESS LIMITED IBADAN

University Press Limited

IBADAN BENIN KANO LAGOS
OWERRI ZARIA

Oxford University Press

OXFORD LONDON GLASGOW
NEW YORK TORONTO MELBOURNE WELLINGTON
KUALA LUMPUR SINGAPORE HONG KONG TOKYO
DELHI BOMBAY CALCUTTA MADRAS KARACHI
NAIROBI DAR ES SALAAM

© Oxford University Press 1978
© University Press Limited 1979

ISBN 0 19 575300 3

Reprinted 1979, 1982

Printed by Academy Press Ltd., Lagos.
Published by University Press Limited
Three Crowns Building, Jericho, P.M.B. 5095, Ibadan, Nigeria

To my parents and children, and
my many benefactors both at home
and abroad

ACKNOWLEDGEMENTS

My indebtedness to earlier writers on the Yoruba Language will be apparent on many of the pages of this book and is readily admitted in the Introduction. Beyond that, I am deeply grateful to my past students at the Universities of Lagos and Ibadan, and my colleagues in those two institutions as well as at the University of Ifẹ. It was the former who first began pressing me to write this book, and they together with the latter helped considerably in their different ways to clarify my thoughts on the language. Lastly, but not in the least, I am grateful to Mr. S. F. Ọdẹbọ who patiently and expertly typed the entire book from manuscript.

TABLE OF CONTENTS

Acknowledgements   vii

Introduction   xiii

1 **Parts of Speech**   1

Language Universality; Language Specificity;
Principle of Classification; Application to Yoruba;
Possible Criteria; Classification by Function;
Comprehension; Exercises

2 **Nouns**   7

Definition; Actual Function; Definition's Implica-
tion; Subject/Object Function; Classification:
Human Nouns; Nonhuman Nouns; Value Nouns;
Quantity Nouns; Demonstrative Nouns; Place
Nouns; Manner Nouns; Relatival Head Nouns;
Genitival Head Nouns; Polymorphic Nouns;
Interrogative Nouns; Count Nouns; Mass Nouns;
Comprehension; Exercises

3 **Qualifiers**   30

Definition; Actual Function; Definition's Implications; Manner of Cooccurrence with Nouns;
Classification: Numerals; Demonstratives; Determiners; Relative Clauses; Adjectives; Appositive
Qualifiers; Genitival Qualifiers; Topical Qualifiers; Interrogative Qualifiers; Cooccurrence of
Qualifiers; Comprehension; Exercises

4 **Verbs**   45

Definition; Actual Function; Definition's Implications; Subject Selection; Object Selection; Classification: Serial Verbs; Splitting Verbs; Echoing

Verbs; Complex Verbs; Adjectivisable Verbs;
Nominal Assimilating Verbs; Particle Selecting
Verbs; Report Verbs; Impersonal Verbs; Causa-
tive Verbs; Symmetrical Verbs; Interrogative
Verbs; Imperative Verbs; Comprehension;
Exercises

5 **Modifiers**   66

Definition; Actual Function; Adverbs and
Adverbials; Classification: Verbal Modifiers; Pre-
Verbal Adverbs; Pre-Verbal Adverbials; Post-
Verbal Adverbs; Post-Verbal Adverbials; Senten-
tials; Sentence-Initial Sententials; Sentence-Final
Sententials; Sentence-Initial/Final Sententials;
Interrogative Modifiers; Obligatory Modifiers;
Comprehension; Exercises

6 **Introducers**   86

Definition and Function; Introducers for Nouns;
Introducers for Qualifiers; The Introducer *Ti;*
The Introducer *Ni;* Introducer for Verbs; Intro-
ducers for Modifiers; The Preposition *Fi;* The
Preposition *Bá;* The Preposition *Ti;* The Preposi-
tion *Sí;* The Preposition *Ni;* The Preposition
Fún; The Preposition *Pẹlú;* The 'Introducer' *Kọ́;*
The Particle *Ni;* Comprehension; Exercises

7 **Conjunctions and Disjunctions**   104

Definition; Actual Function and Characteristics,
Conjunctions; Disjunctions; Comprehension;
Exercises

8 **Sentences**   111

Basic Word Order; Nonbasic Word Order; Verbs
and Sentences: Imperative Sentences; Sentences
with Unspecified Verbs; Serial Verbal Sentences;
Splitting Verb Sentences; Echoing Verb
Sentences; Nominal Assimilating Verb Sentences;
Sentences with the Particle *Ni;* Sentences with
Report Verbs; Sentences with Impersonal Verbs;

Sentences with Symmetrical Verbs; Sentences
with Causative Verbs; Interrogative Sentences;
Sentences with Cognate Objects; Sentences with
Cognate Adverbials; Negative Sentences; Conditional Sentences; Timeless Sentences; Sentences
with Topical Qualifiers; Comprehension; Exercises

9 **Sounds**   136

Sounds and Words; Sounds and Letters; Speech
Organs; Sound Quality; Classification: Tones;
Vowels; Oral Vowels; Nasal Vowels; Back
Vowels; Front Vowels; Central Vowels; Vowel
Height; Consonants; Stops; Fricatives; Other
Consonants; Comprehension; Exercises

10 **Sounds in Combination**   146

The Syllable; The Distribution of Tones; Con-
sonant-Vowel Combinations; The *l* and *n* Alter-
nation; Vowel Harmony; Nasal Vowels and the
Vowel *U;* Contraction; Assimilation; Tone
Change; Comprehension; Exercises

INTRODUCTION

There has existed for quite some time now a keenly felt need for a simple, straightforward, comprehensive, and scientific book on Yoruba grammar for use in Grammar Schools, Colleges, and introductory courses for undergraduates. The present one, it is hoped, will go some way in filling that need.

The book is an abridged version of a much longer work in progress. As such, it contains for the most part and as its title suggests only the barest facts of the structure of the language as perceived by the author in part from his close study of earlier works on the same subject and in part from his own on-going independent research begun almost a decade ago. Not only does the book omit criticisms of traditional misconceptions, detailed arguments, and long proofs, except where they are considered absolutely necessary for comprehension, but, because of its introductory character, it also avoids as much of the technical language of Modern Linguistics as it safely can.

The book attempts to present the grammatical structure of the Yoruba language in a genuinely modern (but not ultramodern) way. For this reason, most readers are going to find in it much that is new or untraditional. For example, the consistent employment of function as the only criterion for establishing the major parts of speech of the language, the claim that words like *kíákíá* (quickly), *wéréwéré* (quickly) are nouns and not adverbs, the claim that all but two of the verbs presently existing in the language are transitive, and the claim that qualifiers always follow the nouns they qualify. Such claims may be new, but they all follow very logically from long-established but easily overlooked facts of the language. Thus, to give one simple example, the word *gbogbo* (entirety) in these two sentences:

Mo ná gbogbo owó náà.   (I spent all the money.)
Mo ná gbogbo rè.   (I spent it all.)

is analysed as a noun in the present book. This analysis was arrived at in the following way:

(a) The word *rè* is a qualifier. (Given/known fact).
(b) This same word is mutually substitutable with *owó náà* in the first sentence; hence *owó náà* is a qualifier also.
(c) Qualifiers occur with nouns only.
(d) The qualifiers *rè* and *owó náà* occur with *gbogbo* in the above sentences.
(e) Therefore, *gbogbo* there is a noun and not an adjective, as popularly believed.

All the other claims in this book have been arrived at in similar fashion and, as much as possible, in full keeping with the four principles of accuracy, completeness, consistency, and simplicity which guide all scientific works. The average reader is not trained to be able to evaluate the technical merits of such claims. Consequently, the only fruitful thing for him to do is to try to understand the rationale behind them. Sporadic hints are given in the book to aid him in such an exercise. In addition to such hints, simple questions designed to aid comprehension, and exercises of varying degrees of difficulty are provided at the end of each chapter. If done conscientiously, most of the exercises are such as would force the reader or student to think for himself about the language, thereby permitting him to gain some insight into how claims made in books of this kind are actually arrived at.

The comprehension questions and exercises provided are not exhaustive, however. They are not meant to be. Instead, they are meant to be suggestive of what a skilful and experienced teacher might do to make his students discover the structural facts of the language for themselves. As such, teachers are expected and urged to supplement them with other exercises made to order for their students.

Another type of novelty in this book is the representation of some grammatical elements; for example *iyín, irè, iwa,* etc. for *yín* (your), *rè* (his), *wa* (our), respectively, and *ó fé 'élo sí apá òhún* for *ó fé lo sí apá òhún*. Such novelties have not been introduced just for the sake of being different, but first and foremost because they are called for within the framework of the present grammatical exposition, and only secondarily because they would at least in theory appreciably simplify the study and teaching of the grammar of the language. Thus, *ó fẹ́ 'ẹ́lọ sí apá ọ̀hún* as just written means only 'He, she, or it wants to go in that direction'. Written as *ó fẹ́ lọ sí apá ọ̀hún*, however, as has been suggested in some quarters, this sentence would not have only the meaning given it earlier, it would also mean 'It blew in that direction'. In other words, the hitherto accepted way of writing the language does not permit the utterance which means 'He, she, it wants to go in that direction' to be orthographically differentiated from the otherwise quite distinct utterance meaning 'It blew in that direction'. It represents these two utterances ambiguously. Spurious ambiguities of this kind, however, create problems for the teacher and the learner alike, as the two of them are forced to strain themselves mentally trying to differentiate the undifferentiated. Given the representation dictated by purely structural and expository considerations in this book, however, spurious ambiguities of the type under consideration and the teaching and learning problems they create will just not arise at all.

The representation of *yín* (your), *rẹ̀* (his, her, its), *wa* (our), etc. as *iyín, irẹ̀, iwa,* respectively, is also dictated by theoretical and expository considerations: such a representation permits a single, simple, and exceptionless rule of assimilation to be formulated to account for identical phenomena which have hitherto been confusingly explained in terms of lengthening, addition or insertion, and assimilation. To the extent that the representation employed in this book avoids this confusion, it makes the teaching and learning of the language easier than before. To this extent also the representation is preferable to the one currently in use.

Interjections have been left out of this exposition because they seem in the present state of knowledge to have no place at all in Yoruba sentence structure. It is assumed that Yoruba dictionaries will carry them just as they carry most idioms. Apart from interjections, any other omissions that may be discovered in this book are unintentional and arise from the author's necessarily incomplete and imperfect knowledge of the whole language.

CHAPTER 1

Parts of Speech

LANGUAGE UNIVERSALITY

1.1 Any given language is made up of syntactic classes of words[1]; that is, words that behave in a similar way in the sentences of the language. Such classes of words are traditionally referred to as parts of speech. The primary job of the grammarian of any language is (1) to establish the number and types of syntactic classes of words in the language, and (2) to describe how individual members of such classes of words are combined to form acceptable sentences or utterances in the language. A good description must be straightforward and easy to follow.

LANGUAGE SPECIFICITY

1.2 There is no fixed number of parts of speech that must be found in every language. In other words, some languages have more parts of speech than others. This being the case, it is no use for someone wanting to find out how many parts of speech there are in Yoruba to look to Hausa, or Igbo, or English for guidance. Such a person must find guidance for himself within the Yoruba language itself and there only.

1.3 To ask how many parts of speech are in Yoruba is to ask how many syntactic classes Yoruba words can be divided or sub-classified into. If Yoruba words can be sub-classified into ten groups, then there are ten parts of speech in the language.

---

[1] Words are sounds or combinations of sounds having meanings.

PRINCIPLE OF CLASSIFICATION

1.4 Things that all look alike cannot be sub-classified. It is only when things differ from one another in some way or manner that they can be sub-classified. Thus, the following set of circles cannot be sub-classified, because they are alike in all ways.

By contrast, the following set can be sub-classfied.

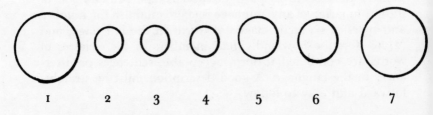

They differ from one another in size. For this reason, they can be sub-classified by size, and only by size, into three classes as follows:

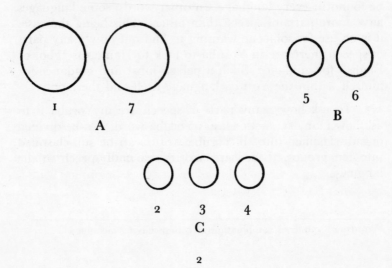

APPLICATION TO YORUBA

1.5 Yoruba words differ from one another. But they do not differ from one another in just one way only, as in the case of the second set of circles above. Words in the language differ from one another in very many ways. They differ in meaning, thus *ilé* means 'house' and *oko* 'farm'. They differ in size, some words being long, e.g. *àgádágodo* 'padlock', and others short, e.g. *ó* (he, it, she). They differ in their beginning and they also differ in their ending. Because Yoruba words differ from one another in so many ways, there are correspondingly many ways in which they can be sub-classified. Not all these ways are useful for writing the grammar of the language, however. They are not all useful because the members of each of the classes of words that some of them yield will not behave alike in Yoruba sentences. And because they will not behave alike, it will not be possible to make general and simple statements about them; in which case, they will not make it possible for simple and straight-forward grammars of the language to be produced.

POSSIBLE CRITERIA

1.6 Only a few of the ways referred to above are generally considered useful for sub-classifying Yoruba words into parts of speech. These are meaning, derivation, syntactic behaviour, and function. Some grammars use meaning alone. Others use combinations of these, such as meaning and derivation, or derivation and function. But no existing Yoruba grammar uses function only.

1.7 A grammar defines its parts of speech on the basis of meaning if it defines nouns, for example, as words signifying persons, places, and things. In a classification based on derivation, nouns again might be defined as words formed by means of *ì-, à,* etc., as in *ìṣe* (deed) and *àlọ* (going). On the other hand, in a classification based on syntactic behaviour, nouns could be defined as words whose ending is prolonged on a mid-tone when followed by a word beginning with a consonant in the following construction:

> ìwée Dàda
> ọkòọ Dàda

Finally, in a classification based on function, nouns would be defined on the basis of the function they actually perform in sentences.

1.8 Classifications on the basis of meaning or derivation or syntactic behaviour, or even on the basis of combinations of these, are of limited value for describing Yoruba grammar. This is so because none of them permits *all* the words in the language to be classified. When such classifications have been completed, it is always found that there are words which still have not been properly classified. Such words are sometimes referred to misleadingly as exceptions.

CLASSIFICATION BY FUNCTION

1.9 The only proper way to classify Yoruba words for syntactic purposes is by the functions that they actually perform in sentences. For this reason, it is not safe to classify words occurring in isolation. People as well as grammars which classify Yoruba words in isolation would not hesitate to say that *lọ* is definitely a verb and nothing else. But they are completely wrong, because we can and do say:

lọ tí o kọ yẹn kò dára tó. (The 'lọ' that you have written is not good enough.)

And in this sentence, *lọ* definitely functions, or is used, as a noun.

Classifications that are not based on function were said above to be of limited value for one reason. Another reason why they are of limited value is that they would not make anyone suspect at all that Yoruba words can be used as in the example just given.

1.10 On the basis of the functions they actually perform in sentences, Yoruba words fall into six major syntactic classes or parts of speech. These parts of speech are: Nouns, Qualifiers, Verbs, Modifiers, Introducers and Conjunctions. These will be defined, discussed, and exemplified in turn in the next six chapters of this book.

4

COMPREHENSION

1. What are parts of speech? What are syntactic classes of words? Are these two the same or different?
2. Name the two primary jobs of a grammarian.
3. 'There is a fixed number of parts of speech to every language.' Is this statement correct?
4. Will a knowledge of Hausa tell someone how many parts of speech are in Yoruba? If not, why not?
5. When are things sub-classifiable: when they are identical or when they are not identical?
6. Are all Yoruba words similar?
7. Name some of the ways in which Yoruba words can be sub-classified.
8. Name the ways in which Yoruba words have actually been sub-classified by grammarians.
9. Name the way Yoruba words are sub-classified in this book.

*EXERCISES

A
   i. If asked to describe your school, you will be expected to mention at least the following: name, location, size and type, students/pupils, teachers.
Do you think it is possible to describe your school just as fully and as accurately without mentioning any of these points? If not, why not?

   ii. Make a list of the things you will mention if asked to describe how a bicycle works.

   iii. Is it possible to describe how a bicycle works without mentioning any one of those things? If not, why not?

   iv. Now think of a reason or of reasons why grammarians always sub-classify Yoruba words into parts of speech as a first step in describing how the language works.

   v. Do you think it is possible to describe how a language works without making use of the idea of parts of speech? If so, suggest some such ways.

B
   i. Which of the following will be useful for sub-classifying all the students in your school into the fewest possible groups: sex, height, class or form or year, hair-style, appearance, weight, complexion, voice and age.

ii. Which of these characteristics do you think is/are unsatisfactory for sub-classifying them? Why do you think so?

iii. How do you know when the job of sub-classifying has been completed?

iv. How do you determine the success or failure of each attempt at sub-classifying them?

v.   Are the classifications based on sex, age, height, and form equally useful?

vi. To which of these would a sub-classification of the students in your school be useful, and why: yourself, the headmaster/principal/registrar, taxi-driver, prefect, post-master, road inspector?

C i.   Pick up a few existing grammars of the language, and find out how words have been sub-classified in them.

ii. Sub-classify all Yoruba words on your own on the basis of each of the following: meaning, appearance, length, derivation (i.e. manner of formation).

iii. Do these four methods yield exactly the same number of sub-classes?

iv. Which of these methods yields sub-classes that are useful for showing how the language works?

v.   What kind of difficulties or problems did you encounter in trying to apply each of these four methods?

CHAPTER 2

Nouns

2.1 Any word functioning as the subject of a verb or the object of a verb or preposition[1] in a grammatical sentence in the language is a noun.

ACTUAL FUNCTION

2.2 Subject indicates the performer of the action referred to in a sentence. Thus in,

Òjó ra ìwé.   (Ojo bought books.)

Òjó is subject, because it represents the person that performed the action of buying books.

2.3 Object of verbs indicates the person, thing, etc., that action was, or is to be, performed upon in a sentence. Hence, in the sentence:

Òjó lu Dàda.   (Ojo beat Dada.)

Dàda is object, since it represents the person on whom the action of beating was performed.

2.4 Object of prepositions indicates many kinds of ideas or concepts such as time, location, condition, etc. The following words function as object of prepositions in the sentences given below:

oko	(farm)
ibẹ	(there)
kíákíá	(quickly)
ṣíṣí	(open state)

---

[1]Prepositions are discussed in Chapter 6 below.

Mo lọ sí oko.	(I went to the farm.)
Ó wà ní ibẹ̀.	(He was there.)
Ó jáde ní kíákíá.	(He went out without delay.)
Fèrèsé náà wà ní ṣíṣí.	(The window is open.)

DEFINITION'S IMPLICATION

2.5 According to the definition given above, all the words referred to in other grammars of the language as nouns are indeed nouns. Examples of such words are:

ọjà	(market)	oko	(farm)
owó	(money)	àlàáfíà	(peace, good health)
èrò	(thought)	àtúnṣe	(correction)

2.6 However, there are many words which those grammars say are not nouns but which are, in fact, nouns, because they function as specified in the above definition. Examples are:

títí	(period)	pẹlẹbẹ	(flat)
bí	(manner)	gbọ̀n-ọ́ngbọ̀n-ọ́n	?
kàkà	(instead of)	ta	(who?)
gẹ́gẹ́	(coincidence)	kí	(what?)
roboto	(round)	ti	(possession)
dípò	(instead of)		

Kò lọ títí (tí) mo fi dé.	(He didn't leave until I got back.)
Ṣe bí mo ti wí.	(Do as I say.)
Kàkà tí ì bá fi lọ, ó ń ṣe ìranù.	(He fooled around instead of going there.)
Dípò tí ì bá fi lọ, ó ń ṣe ìranù.	(He fooled around instead of going there.)
Fìlà yí ṣe gẹ́gẹ́ orí mi.	(This cap fits my head.)
Ó rí roboto.	(It is round.)
Ó ṣe pẹlẹbẹ.	(It is flat.)
Ó ta gbọ̀n-ọ́ngbọ̀n-ọ́n.	(He stumbled.)
Ta ni ìyẹn?	(Who is that?)
Kí ni ìyẹn?	(What is that?)
Ti Òjó dà.	(Where is Ojo's own?)

8

The words *títí, bí, kàkà,* and *dípò* are each accompanied by a relative clause qualifier in the first four of these examples. As will be pointed out in the next chapter, qualifiers co-occur with nouns only. (Anything that is not a noun will first have to be turned into a noun before a qualifier can be attached to it). Their co-occurrence here with the four words listed above is an indirect proof that the words themselves are nouns. Those four words, together with their qualifiers, function in the above examples as the object of the preposition *ní.* (The preposition is not actually present there, because it has been deleted; see **5.20, 5.21, 5.30,** and **5.31,** below). Hence they fulfil the only condition laid down for their being classified as nouns under the above definition. ,

In the next four examples, *gégé, roboto, pèlèbè* and *gbòòngbòòn* each functions as the object of a deleted preposition *ní.* For more on this, see **2.9, 2.18, 5.20** and **5.21,** below.

Ta and *kí* in the next two examples are the object of the verb *jé* (be) or *şe* (be) which has been deleted. Hence, those sentences can also occur as:

Ta ni ìyẹn ń şe?   (Who is that?)
Kí ni ìyẹn jé?   (What is that?)

For more on this, see **8.14,** below.

2.7 Besides the words just exemplified, the following words normally function only as nouns, with the exception of *gbogbo* which can also function as a qualifier.

gbogbo		(entirety, whole, all)	
ogún, ọgbòn, ogójì, etc.		(twenty, thirty, forty, etc)	
kìkì	(only)	ààbò	(half)
şàşà	(few)	ogúnlógò	(several)
òfo	(empty)	òpò	(many)
ìdáàjì	(half)	àwọn	(entities)

Anyone who takes the time to study the way all these words are actually used in Yoruba sentences will find that they function as subject and/or object. They are normally accompanied by qualifiers in either of these functions (Cf. **2.20** and **3.5,** below). For example,

9

Ó jí gbogbo rẹ̀.	(He stole all of it.)
Ó fẹ́ ogún iṣu.	(He wanted twenty yams.)
Ṣàṣà wọn ni ó mọ ibẹ̀.	(Only a few of them know the place.)
Òfo ìgò pọ̀ ní ibẹ̀.	(There are many empty bottles there.)
Àwọn kan kò dára.	(Some are not good.)

2.8 Another class of words which other grammars fail to recognize as nouns consists of all the words or sounds in the language besides the ones already referred to. Practically any word in the language can be used as a noun, depending upon the situation. Because they can be so used, they are potential nouns. Thus, the sounds represented by *t, b, m*, etc. and *wá, mọ̀, ṣe, mọ́, kò pẹ́*, etc. are all potential nouns. They become actual nouns, however, only when they are used with or without accompanying qualifiers in the functions of subject and/or object, as in:

Olùkọ́ wa kọ 'b' àti 'wá'.	(Our teacher wrote 'b' and 'wá'.)
'wá' rẹ̀ kò dára.	(His 'wá' was not good.)
'b' tí ó kọ wọ́.	(The 'b' he wrote wasn't straight.)
'Kò pẹ́ rẹ̀ ni wọn dé [ìdí] tábìlì...' [1]	('They were at table shortly after that'.)

SUBJECT/OBJECT FUNCTION

2.9 Most of the nouns in the language can function as subject and object of verbs. A few nouns, however, normally never function in that way. Instead, they function as object of prepositions, particularly of the preposition *ní*. Such nouns are, for example,

ọgán	(suddenness)	mẹ́fàmẹ́fà	(six by six)
òjijì	(suddenness)	kíákíá	(quickly)
ọ̀sọ̀ọ̀sẹ̀	(weekly)	wéréwéré	(quickly)
oṣooṣù	(monthly)	júujùu	(disorder)

---

[1] Awoniyi, T. A., *Aiyé Kòótọ́*, Ibadan: Onibọnoje Press, 1973, p. 6.

ẹsẹẹsẹ	(row by row)	gẹlẹtẹ	(idle, not doing anything)
méjìméjì	(two by two)	pẹlẹbẹ	(thin and flat)

Ó dé ní ọgán.	(He returned suddenly.)
Ó ń wá ní òsòòsè.	(He comes weekly.)
Ó ń mú wọn ní méjìméjì.	(He takes them two at a time.)
Ó jáde ní wéréwéré.	(He came out quickly.)
iṣu tí a bẹ ní pẹlẹbẹ pẹlẹbẹ[1]	(yam that is sliced thin)

For more on these nouns, see **2.18** and **3.3**, below.

CLASSIFICATION

2.10 The number of nouns in the language is infinite. This is because there exist in the language processes for forming new nouns at will, thereby adding to their number. It is convenient to discuss such processes in Chapter 6 (See Sections **6.4—6.13** below).

2.11 There is no easy way to subdivide the nouns in the language. In other words, different writers are likely to subdivide them differently, depending upon the criteria they use. In the present book, a combination of meaning and syntactic behaviour is used to arrive at the following subclasses of nouns.[2]

2.12 Human Nouns
Examples:

Òjó	(Ojo)	tíṣà	(Teacher)	mo	(I)
Dàda	(Dada)	èmi	(I)	adájó	(judge)
Ọba	(king)	òun/ó	(He, She)	ta	(who?)

Ta ni?	(Who is it?)
Èmi ni.	(It's me.)

---

[1] Adeboye Babalọla, *Àkójọpọ̀ Àlọ́ Ìjàpá* Apá Kìnní, OUP., 1973, p. 169. Cf. *nwọ́n sì rí òmìràn náà tí ó gé sí wẹ́lẹwẹ̀lẹ* (They saw the giant break up into bits and pieces). D.O. Fagunwa, *Itan Oloyin*, OUP., 1963, p. 16.

[2] Precise names have not yet been found for all the classes of nouns set up here. For this reason, the names suggested should not all be taken literally. This is particularly advisable in the case of manner nouns in **2.18** below.

All the words in this class refer to human beings. Twelve of them are differentiated for number (singular-plural) and person (1st, 2nd, 3rd). Of those twelve, six are given in the table below, and the remaining six in Section **2.21**, under Polymorphic Nouns.

	SINGULAR	PLURAL
1ST PERSON	Èmi	Àwa
2ND PERSON	Ìwọ	Ẹ̀yin
3RD PERSON	Òun	Àwọn

The present class of human nouns contains what are traditionally known as 'proper nouns' and 'pronouns'. That these two traditional classes have to be combined into just one, as done here, is shown by the fact that both the so-called proper nouns and the so-called pronouns are questioned alike by means of the noun *ta* (who?) (see **2.22**, below).

The six nouns given in the above table are traditionally known as 'emphatic pronouns'. In fact, however, apart from the fact that they are differentiated for number and person, they are no different from traditional nouns. Thus, like traditional nouns, they function as subject and object; they occur with a wide variety of qualifiers; low-tone monosyllabic verbs change their tone to mid-tone before them; and a high-tone syllable occurs between them and verbs when they function as subject (see **4.7**, below). Given these considerations, it has not seemed useful at all to recognize a class of emphatic pronouns as distinct from nouns, once it has been stated for such 'pronouns' that they are differentiated as already indicated.

The so-called unemphatic pronouns, too, are nouns as defined in this chapter. Moreover, they are human nouns in most of their meanings. (*Ó* is non-human when it means 'it'.) But they also form a subclass of their own (see **2.21**, below) because of their forms, of the fact that they never take qualifiers (see **2.21**), of the fact that most of them exclude 'the high-tone syllable' when functioning as subject (see **4.7**, and **5.11**, below), and of the fact that low-tone monosyllabic verbs do not change their tone before them as object nouns (see **4.10**, below).

It is thought' that 'pronouns stand for nouns' and are therefore different from nouns. This is the wrong reason, however, for separating 'pronouns' from nouns; for some nouns regularly 'stand for' other nouns and it has never occurred to anyone to call such nouns pronouns. For example, the noun *ìgbà* or *àkókò* (time) can stand for such times as *àárò* (morning), *agogo méfà* (six o'clock), *agogo kan* (one o'clock). Similarly, *okùnrin* (man) can 'stand for' *Òjó, Àmódù, Akin, Sùbérù*, etc., just as *èniyàn* (person) can 'stand for' *Dàda, Èmi 'Í', Òjó, Àíná, Bísí*, etc. The logic of distinguishing between nouns and 'pronouns' on the grounds that the latter 'stand for nouns' would require that *ìgbà* or *àkókò* (time), *okùnrin* (man), *èniyàn* (human-being, person) in the above examples be classified as pronouns rather than as nouns. But no one would want to do so, and in that case, no one should logically wish to differentiate between nouns and 'pronouns' merely on the grounds that the latter 'stand for nouns'.

At best, the so-called pronouns constitute sub-classes of human nouns. It has, however, not been considered useful to recognize more than one such sub-class in this book. For that sub-class, see **2.21**, below.

2.13 Non-Human Nouns

Examples:

èní	(today)	òun/ó	(it)
èjì, eéjì	(two)	eranko	(animal)
àìmò	(ignorance)	kí	(what?)
kiní	(thing)	pé kí á sóra	(that we must be careful)
eye	(bird)	ìséjú	(minute)

Kí ni?	(What is it?)
Eye ni.	(It's a bird.)

The nouns in this sub-class refer to things other than human-beings. They are questioned by means of the noun *kí* (what?).

Human and non-human represent two of the four most basic sub-classifications of Yoruba nouns: any noun in the language has to be, in any given context, a member of either one or the other of these two sub-classes. (For the remaining two most basic sub-classes, see **2.23—2.25**, below).

Notice that, in normal everyday usage, human nouns are questioned with the noun *kí* (what?) to show contempt for the person involved. Thus, when one says:

Kí ni ó ń sọ̀rọ̀ ní 'bẹ̀ yẹn?   (What is making noise there?)
one is showing how little regard he has for the individual being addressed.

2.14   Value Nouns

Examples:

kọ́bọ̀	(kobo)	àpò	(£100 or ₦200)
Náírà	(Naira)	ẹgbẹ̀rin	(two and a half pence, 2½d)
tọ́rọ́	(three-pence)	ẹgbàarùn-ún	(2s.6d. or 25k)
sísì	(six pence, five kobo)	èló	(how much?)
ṣílè	(shilling, ten kobo)	ọ̀kẹ́	(5s. or 50k)

Èló ni?   (How much is it?)
Sísì ni.   (It's five kobo.)

The nouns in this class refer to sums of money. They are questioned by means of the noun *èló* (how much?). In everyday usage, they are most commonly preceded by the 'particle' *ní* (see **6.40**, below). For example,

Mo rà á ní kọ́bọ̀ mẹ́wàá.   (I paid ten kobo for it.)
Mo tà á ní náírà kan.   (I sold it for one Naira.)
Yá mi ní kọ́bọ̀ kan.   (Please, lend me one kobo.)
Ó jẹ mi ní àpò kan.   (He owes me ₦200.)

For more on these kinds of sentences, see **8.10**, and **8.20**, below.

2.15   Quantity Nouns

Examples:

ìkan	(one)	ọgbọ̀n	(thirty)
mélòó	(how many?)	irínwó	(four hundred)
mẹ́ta	(three)	ẹgbẹ̀ta	(six hundred)

Mélòó ni?   (How many are they?)
Mẹ́fà ni.   (They are six.)

Nouns in the above class refer to numerals. They are questioned by means of the noun *mélòó* (how many?). All the nouns in the class, with the possible exception of the ones listed below, are derived:

ọ̀kan/ìkan	(one)	ẹ̀rin	(four)	ẹ̀jọ	(eight)
ení/iní	(one)	àrún	(five)	ẹ̀sán	(nine)
ẹ̀jì	(two)	ẹ̀fà	(six)	ẹ̀wá	(ten)
ẹ̀ta	(three)	èje	(seven)	ogún	(twenty)
				ọgbọ̀n	(thirty)

Those of the nouns beginning with the consonantal sound *m*, e.g. *méjì* (two) seem to be made up of a now obsolete word (probably a verb *mú*) and the nouns *ọ̀kan* (one)..*ẹ̀wá* (ten). This can be partially inferred from the way they are actually pronounced. (For a full discussion and illustration of the formation of quantity nouns, see any good traditional grammar of the language).

The nouns *ení* (one) ... *ẹ̀wá* (ten) are reserved in everyday usage almost exclusively for counting. Occasionally, however, they function as object. For example, in

Ìyẹn ení/iní   (That makes one.)

which is a shortened form of

Ìyẹn jẹ́ ení/iní   (That makes one.)

It does not appear that they function as subject in the standard form of the language, except in the formation of other quantity nouns e.g. *ẹ̀jìdínlógún,* which is *ẹ̀jì í dín ní ogún* lit. 'two are missing from twenty', i.e. 'eighteen'.

2.16 Demonstrative Nouns

Examples:

èyí	(this one)	dúdú	(the black one)
ìyẹn	(that one)	funfun	(the white one)
ìkínní	(the first one)	èwo	(which one?)

Èwo ni?   (Which one is it?)
Ìyẹn ni.   (It's that one.)

Most of the nouns in this sub-class are derived from qualifiers; that is, in other words, they are qualifiers made to function as nouns. They are characteristically used to specify or point out elements, rather than merely to name them. They are questioned by means of the noun *èwo* (which one?).

2.17 Place Nouns

Examples:

ibi	(place, location)	bí/bá	(manner, way)
ibí	(here)	kí	(what?)
ọjà	(market)	ọ̀dọ̀	(presence)
ọ̀nà	(road, way, method)		

Kí ni wọn ti şe é?	(How did they do it?)
Şé bí wọn ti şe é?	(You mean how they did it?)
Ibi tí wọn ti şe é.	(Where they did it)

With the exception of *bí/bá* (manner, way) and *kí* (what?) the nouns in this class as a rule refer to places or locations. The actual distinguishing feature of the class as a whole is that, in certain easily specifiable contexts (see **6.22** below), relative clause qualifiers or topical qualifiers (see **3.12** and **3.16** below), qualifying them display the preposition *ti*. This is true of all the three examples given above.

Some people regularly leave out such a preposition from some expressions other than the ones given here. For example,

Ibẹ̀ ni ó bá mi.	(He found me there.)

instead of

Ibẹ̀ ni ó ti bá mi.	(He found me there.)

That the preposition should not be left out is shown, however, by the fact that there is a world of difference (e.g., for a detainee or prisoner) between the following:

Àárín ọgbà ni kí o rìn.	(Go through the middle of the yard.)
Àárín ọgbà ni kí o ti rìn.	(Walk/stroll in the middle of the yard.)

2.18 Manner Nouns

Examples:

bí/bá	(manner, way)	kólíẹ́	(tiny)
títí	(period)	fòò	(red manner)
ọgán	(suddenness)	òkòòkan	(one by one)
òjijì	(suddenness)	ojoojúmọ́	(day by day)
kíákíá	(quick manner)	ẹyẹẹyọ	(piece by piece)
díẹ̀díẹ̀	(little by little)	ẹsẹẹsẹ	(line by line)
kìtàkìtà	(no convenient English translation)		

Ṣe pẹ̀lẹ́pẹ̀lẹ́.	(Be careful.)
Ó ń fì dùgbẹ̀dùgbẹ̀	(It's swaying heavily.)
Ó dé ní òjijì.	(He arrived without warning.)
Mo wò ó títí.	(I kept looking at him for a long while.)
Wọn ń lé 'ra wọn kìtàkìtà	(They pursued themselves with heavy footsteps.)

The vast majority of the words here called nouns are referred to as adverbs or adjectives in existing grammars of the language. For example,

Ó rí roboto.	(It is round.)
Ó dé kíákíá.	(He quickly returned.)

This popular view cannot be correct, however, for two reasons. First, *roboto* and *kíákíá* cannot be adjectives in the above two sentences because they do not qualify any nouns there, as every adjective must do (see Chapter 3). They are not adverbs either. Adverbs cannot be moved from their places of occurrence. Thus the following,

Ó tètè lọ.	(He left without delay.)
Ó lọ rí.	(He has gone before.)

in which *tètè* and *rí* are adverbs, cannot be turned into:

* tètè ni ó lọ.
* rí ni ó lọ.

(These sentences are marked with asterisks to indicate that they are unacceptable). By contrast, words like *kíákíá* and *roboto* can be moved from their place of occurrence, as can be seen in:

Roboto ni ó rí.	(It is round.)
Kíákíá ní ó dé.	(He quickly returned.)

17

Second, the traditional view that words like *roboto* and *kíákíá* are adverbs or adjectives cannot be correct because it overlooks a very important piece of evidence contained in sentences like the following:

'Wọn gbẹ́ 'gi ní palaba.' — (They carved wood into a flat shape.)

'Ìmàrò dá aṣọ ní pelebe.' — (The christian sewed the garment too short.)

'Ayé sì wà ní júujùu.' — (Disorder reigned on earth then.)

'Onílé ṣe mí ń (=ní) pẹ̀lẹ́.' — (Dear host, treat me gently.)

'Fátólú ṣan 'ra ní bàràbàrà tán. . .' — (After Fatolu had washed off hurriedly. . .)

'Àrìrà òkè tí í sọlẹ̀ ní kùù.' — (The hoverer that hits the ground with a thud.)

'Ohun tí a ń wádìí wá yé wa ní yékéyéké.' — (What we had been investigating thereupon became crystal clear.)

'Egúngún ò níí lọ ní goloto.' — (The masquerader will not depart nude.)

Ó dé ní kíákíá. — (He quickly returned.)

Ayé ń lọ ní mẹ̀lọmẹ̀lọ. — (Guarded conditions prevailed.)

The words preceded by the preposition *ní* in these examples definitely are nouns, given the definition in **2.1,** above. If they are nouns, then it is necessary to find out what words like *ségesège, jẹ́ẹ́jẹ́, dìẹ̀dìẹ̀, fòò, kìtàkìtà,* etc. really are. In this connection notice that these latter words are exactly like the ones in the above sentences both from the standpoint of the way they sound and from the standpoint of the kinds of meanings they convey. This being the case, one could not classify those in the above sentences as one thing and those listed above in this same paragraph as another. To do so would be to deny the existence of the similarities just pointed out between them. Since those similarities cannot be denied, any grammar of the language must reflect them, and the only way to reflect them is to classify the two sets of words in question as members of the same part of speech.

The question now is: what part of speech? They cannot be classified as adverbs, firstly because some of them are already known to be nouns, and secondly because, as already pointed out, they do not behave like adverbs anyway. As a matter of fact, the simplest analysis or classification of all the words in question is as nouns. If they are all classified as nouns, it would follow that they can be used as in the above examples for the simple and most natural reason that they are nouns. It would also mean that all such words are nouns even in sentences where they are not preceded by the preposition *ní*, as in:

Ṣe ni mo jókòó jẹ́ẹ́jẹ́.   (What happened was that I sat down without molesting anyone.)

This latter conclusion would seem to be right. For sentences like the following, which have hitherto universally been overlooked, in fact exist in the language:

Ṣe ni mo jókòó jẹ́ẹ́jẹ́ mi.   (What happened was that I sat down, as is my habit, without molesting anyone.)

Notice in the sentence that the word *jẹ́ẹ́jẹ́* is not preceded by the preposition *ní*. Notice also that the same word *jẹ́ẹ́jẹ́* is qualified by the qualifier *mi* (my). This would not have been possible if *jẹ́ẹ́jẹ́* were not a noun. (For more on this, see **3.3** below).

The leaving out of the preposition *ní* before nouns like *jẹ́ẹ́jẹ́, kíákíá, kìtàkìtà, fòò, fíofío*, etc. is nothing unusual. In other words, the preposition is not left out before this class of nouns only; it is left out before other classes of nouns also, such as *ìhòhò* (nudity) and *tòótọ́* (= ti òtítọ́) (truth), as in:

Ó rìn 'hòhò.   (He went nude.)
Ó mọ̀ tòótọ́.   (He in fact knows.)

For more on the dropping of the preposition *ní*, see **5.20, 5.21, 5.30,** and **5.31** below.

Any alternative analysis of Yoruba grammar in which words like *kíákíá, jẹ́ẹ́jẹ́, dùgbẹ̀dùgbẹ̀, fíofío*, etc. are not considered as nouns would be extremely complex. This would be the case because such an analysis would have no simple and no real explanation at all for utterances in which such words are either preceded by the preposition *ní* or are accompanied by qualifiers. Such an analysis would only be able to term or label utterances like that as exceptions, which is in reality no explanation at all.

The members of the sub-class of manner nouns normally function only as part of adverbials or adverbial phrases, and it is solely for this reason that they are here referred to, perhaps somewhat imprecisely, as Manner Nouns.

2.19   Relatival Head Nouns

The following is a complete or practically complete list of the nouns in this sub-class:

títí	(while, until)	èyí	(instead)
ìdí	(reason)	kàkà	(instead)
ìgbà	(time)		

Ìgbà tí mo fi máa dé 'bè...	(By the time I got there...)
Èyí tí ò bá fi lọ wéré...	(Instead of going without delay...)
Ìdí tí o fi pè mí l'ọbọ...	(Why you call me a fool...)

Most of these nouns tend normally to be used only with relative clause qualifiers in their meanings or senses given here.

This class of relatival head nouns, it should be noted, is at present not as firmly established as the other classes of nouns already exemplified. The class may turn out, with further research, to be completely unnecessary in the grammar of the language. But that will depend strictly on whether some better way can be found to explain or account for the illustrative phrases given above. There is something definitely peculiar, though somewhat difficult to pinpoint at present, about those phrases. Notice in the first place, that they always contain the preposition *fi*. Secondly, unlike regular phrases containing the preposition *fi*, they seldom, if ever, occur in the following forms:

?	Mo fi ìgbà máa dé ibè.
?	Ò bá fi èyí lọ wéré.
?	O fi ìdí pè mí ní ọbọ.

(The question marks preceding these sentences indicate that they are of doubtful grammatical status). By contrast, the following regular phrase containing the preposition *fi*,

    òbẹ tí mo fi gé e   (The knife I cut it with.)

corresponds to the grammatical sentence:

    Mo fi òbẹ gé e.   (I cut it with a knife.)

2.20 Genitival Head Nouns

The nouns in this class are:

ẹ̀bá	(vicinity)	kìkì	(only)
òdọ̀	(presence)	ti	(possession, own)
gbogbo	(entirety)	ìdá	(essence)
ṣàṣà	(few)		

These nouns function as heads of genitival phrases (see Chapter 3, Section **3.15**) only. As such, they form a distinct sub-class since no other nouns in the language appear to be restricted in this fashion.

Examples of genitival phrases are:

gbogbo iṣu náà	(all the yam)
ti Òjó	(Ojo's own)
òdọ̀ mi	(my presence)
ṣàṣà wọn	(a few of them)
kìkì ìdá agbára	(strength alone)
ìdá kìkì agbára	(strength alone)
kìkì ìdá rẹ̀	(it alone)

Notice that *òdọ̀* (presence) is sometimes used without any accompanying genitival qualifier. For example,

Ó fi ọmọ sí òdọ̀.   (He has a boy/girl living with him and working for him.)

But this sentence is always understood only as a shortened form of:

Ó fi ọmọ sí òdọ̀ ara rẹ̀.   (He has a houseboy/house-girl with himself.)

That is, no one would normally interpret the shorter sentence as meaning:

Ó fi ọmọ sí ọ̀dọ̀ ẹnìkan.   (He has his child living with someone else.)

2.21 Polymorphic Nouns

There are six nouns in this class. Most of them have three different forms that they take when functioning as subject, object, and genitival qualifiers (see Chapter 3); hence their name. Those forms are given below:

		Subject	Object	Genitival Qualifier
SINGULAR	1	mo	mi	ìmi
	2	o	ẹ	ìrẹ
	3	ó	i	irẹ̀
PLURAL	1	a	wa	iwa
	2	ẹ	yín/iyín	iyín
	3	wọn	wọn	iwọn

The six nouns in this class always function as subjects and objects without the help of qualifiers. That is, they never occur with qualifiers at all, unlike the related nouns *èmi*, *ìwọ*, *òun*, *àwa*, *ẹ̀yin*, and *àwọn*, which do.

The six nouns form three pairs of singular and plural nouns, and they are also differentiated for person, as follows:

Subject

	Singular	Plural
1ST PERSON	mo	a
2ND PERSON	o	ẹ
3RD PERSON	ó	wọn

Object

	Singular	Plural
1ST PERSON	mi	wa
2ND PERSON	ẹ	yín/iyín
3RD PERSON	i	wọn

These, together with six related nouns in the class of human nouns (namely: *èmi, ìwọ, òun, àwa, èyin, àwọn*), are the only nouns in the language which can be recognized in isolation as definitely either singular or plural. All other nouns may be either singular or plural, depending upon the context in which they occur.

Special subject forms of the polymorphic nouns are used before some adverbs, as follows:

i. Before *óò* (will, shall)
Subject

	Singular	*Plural*
1ST PERSON	n	a
2ND PERSON	o	ẹ
3RD PERSON	(nothing)	wọn

ii. Before *á* (will, shall)
Subject

	Singular	*Plural*	
1ST PERSON	mà	à	
2ND PERSON	wà	è	(with *á* (will) changed to *ẹ́* (will, shall)
3RD PERSON	á	wọ́n	

iii. Before *ì* (should (have), unaccomplished action)
This adverb and the noun fuse together to become:
Subject

	Singular	*Plural*	
1ST PERSON	ṁ	à	
2ND PERSON	ò	è	
3RD PERSON	(nothing)	wòn/wọn	(i.e. fusing may or may not occur in the case of this noun)

iv. Before *kò* (not)
Subject

	Singular	*Plural*
1ST PERSON	n	a
2ND PERSON	o	ẹ
3RD PERSON	(nothing)	wọn

v. Before *ì* (not) (actual form changes with the context)
Subject

	Singular	Plural
1ST PERSON	mi	a
2ND PERSON	o	ẹ
3RD PERSON	(nothing)	wọn

vi. Before *ò* (not)
Subject

	Singular	Plural
1ST PERSON	mi	a
2ND PERSON	o	ẹ
3RD PERSON	(nothing)	wọn

When the 3rd person singular subject noun *ó* is not represented by anything, only the full form of the negative adverb *kò/kì* (not) must be used. See **8.28** below.

It is not usual to employ polymorphic nouns as subject before the adverb *yóò*. Thus the sentence:

Wọn yóò lọ.   (They will go.)

sounds somewhat inelegant.

The basic form of the 3rd person singular object noun is *i*.[1] This basic form, however, changes with the context: it takes the same form as the vowel of any verb or preposition immediately preceding it. This can be seen in the following examples:

Ó rí i.   (He saw it.)
Ó ṣe é.   (He did it.)
Ó tẹ̀ ẹ́.   (He stepped upon it.)
Ó pa á.   (He killed it.)
Ó kọ̀ ọ́.   (He refused it.)
Ó pò ó.   (He mixed it.)
Ó mú un.   (He took it.)

The object forms of the nouns in the polymorphic class, with the exception of *yín/iyín*, change their tone from mid to

---

[1] The clue to this is in the way the noun changes its form with the context. Normally, only the vowel *i* changes its form like that in the language. Cf. **10.23** below. There are practical as well as theoretical advantages in giving this noun its own unique shape or form, as for the other nouns in the same class. But a discussion of such advantages is definitely beyond the scope of the present book.

high when the preceding monosyllabic verb or preposition has a low-tone or a mid-tone. For example:

Ó rí mi.	(He saw me.)	Ó rí wa.	(He saw us.)
Ó pè mí.	(He called me.)	Ó pè wá.	(He called us.)
Ó bi mí.	(He asked me.)	Ó bi wá.	(He asked us.)

The second person plural noun has two forms, namely, *yín* and *iyín*. The latter form occurs after verbs or prepositions with a high tone, and the former elsewhere. The initial sound of *iyín* changes with the context. For example:

Ó rí iyín.	(He saw you.)
Ó pè yín.	(He called you.)
Ó bi yín.	(He asked you.)
Ó lé eyín.	(He chased you away.)
Ó bẹ̀ yín	(He begged you.)
Ó dẹ yín	(He instigated you.)

The forms that the nouns in the polymorphic class assume when they function as genitival qualifiers change with the contexts in which they occur. But examples of such changes are better given under Genitival Qualifiers in Chapter 3 (see Section **3.15** below). For more on the peculiarities of the polymorphic nouns, see **3.16, 4.7** and **4.10** below, and **2.12** above.

2.22 Interrogative Nouns
There are only five nouns in this sub-class. All of them have interrogative meanings, which is the reason for labelling them as interrogative nouns. They are used for asking questions about members of five of the sub-classes of nouns already exemplified. They combine this interrogative function with their normal function as subject and/or object.

ta	(who?)	for questioning	Human Nouns
kí	(what?)	,,	Non-human Nouns
èwo	(which one?)	,,	Demonstrative Nouns
èló	(how much?)	,,	Value Nouns
mélòó	(how many?)	,,	Quantity Nouns

Ta ni o rí?   (Whom did you see?)
Kí ní o ń wá?   (What are you looking for?)
Èwo ni o fẹ́?   (Which one do you want?)
Èló ni o fẹ́?   (How much do you want?)
Mélòó ni o mú?   (How many did you take?)

2.23 Count Nouns

The nouns in this class are those that can be counted, as shown by the fact that numerals (see Section **3.9** below) can co-occur with them. Some such nouns are:

ilé	(house)	igi	(tree)
ọkọ̀	(vehicle)	ẹyẹ	(bird)
àga	(chair)	ọ̀nà	(road, path)
ọmọ	(child)	ọjà	(market)
ìlú	(town)	èrò	(thought)

Ó ní tó ilé mẹ́fà.   (He owns up to six houses.)
Kò bí ọmọ púpọ̀.   (He did not have many children.)
Mo ra àga mẹ́wàá.   (I bought ten chairs.)
Igi mélòó ni o gé?   (How many trees did you fell?)

2.24 Mass Nouns

Mass nouns cannot be (or are not normally) counted. They are, therefore, the opposite of count nouns. They are questioned differently from count nouns. Some mass nouns in the language are:

àlàáfíà	(good health, peace)	oúnjẹ	(food)
omi	(water)	ọbẹ̀	(stew, soup)
epo	(oil)	ìyà	(suffering)
òjò	(rain)	afẹ́fẹ́	(air)
eérú	(ashes)	ẹmu	(palm wine)

Mass nouns are normally used with the adjectives *díẹ̀* (a little, some), *kékeré* (small, little), and *púpọ̀* (a lot, a great deal).

For example:
Mo mu ẹmu díẹ̀.   (I drank some palm wine.)
Ìyà púpọ̀ ni ó jẹ ẹ́.   (He suffered a great deal.)
Oúnjẹ kékeré kọ́ ni ó jẹ.   (He ate a lot of food.)
Báwo ni oúnjẹ náà ti tóbi tó? (How much food was it?)

26

2.25 Just as every noun in the language is either human or non-human in any given context (see **2.13**), so, too, it is either countable or uncountable; that is, either a count noun or a mass noun. The phrase 'in any given context' is extremely important in the statement just made. What it really means is that, there may be some contexts where a given noun is human (or countable) and some other contexts where the same noun is non-human (or uncountable). For example:

Fún mi ní okùn díẹ̀.   (Give me some length of rope.)
Fún mi ní okùn méjì.   (Give me two pieces of rope.)

In the first sentence *okùn* is a mass noun, whereas in the second sentence it is a count noun. Similarly, in the first sentence below *ọba* is a human noun while it is non-human in the second.

Ọba ni ó ń sọ̀rọ̀.   (It's the king who is speaking.)
N ò fẹ́ jẹ ọba o   (I don't want to be king.)

Cf. also

Akápò ni ó ń sọ̀rọ̀.   (It's the treasurer who is speak-
                           ing.)
Èmi ò fẹ́ jẹ akápò ní   (As for me, I don't want to be
    t'èmi o.   treasurer.)

COMPREHENSION

1. What functions do nouns perform?
2. Does the present book recognize fewer or more nouns in Yoruba than earlier books?
3. Mention ten words which this book calls nouns, but which other books do not call nouns.
4. Why are such words called nouns here?
5. What are potential nouns?
6. How many nouns are in the language?
7. How many sub-classes of nouns are proposed here? Name them.
8. How were they arrived at?
9. Are these all the possible sub-classes of nouns in the language?

10. What nouns are referred to as polymorphic? Why are they said to be polymorphic?

EXERCISES

A Study the following definition of Yoruba nouns carefully and answer the questions based on it:

> 'A word which gives a name to an individual person, a thing or a place is called a noun. The term 'noun' is also given to words which grammatically behave like nouns.'

1. What kind of definition is this—a semantic (i.e. based on meaning) definition or a grammatical one or both?
2. Is it a uniform definition of nouns? If not, why not?
3. The definition implies that some Yoruba nouns do not give names to individual persons, things, or places. Name a few such nouns.
4. Why is the second part of the definition necessary?
5. Does the first part say how nouns behave grammatically in the language?
6. What differences are there between this definition and the one given at the beginning of this Chapter?

B Identify the subject and/or object in the following sentences:

1. Mo ti ṣe iṣẹ́ náà.   (I have done the work.)
2. Ẹ̀rù kò bà mí rárá.   (I wasn't afraid at all.)
3. Ẹ bá mi pe Òjó.   (Call Ojo for me.)
4. Mo lá àlá ní àná.   (I had a dream yesterday.)
5. Epo ni mo rà.   (Oil is what I bought.)
6. Owó kò sí ní ọwọ́ mi.   (I have no money on me.)
7. Ṣé kò sí nǹkan?   (Is anything the matter?)
8. Mo mọ ọkọ̀ wà.   (I can drive.)
9. Ìwé tí o rà dà?   (Where is the book you bought?)
10. Wọ́n ba ọkọ̀ náà jẹ́.   (They damaged the vehicle.)

28

C Look for and find (by asking people) as many other sentences like the following as you can:

Ó dé ní kíákíá.

Consult Yoruba books also, as they occur there; e.g. in *Ẹ̀ṣin Atiroja* by Ọlanipẹkun Ẹsan.

D Use the following words in sentences in such a way as to show clearly that they are nouns: *gbogbo, kìkì, ṣàṣà, pẹlẹbẹ, játijàti, ẹ̀ẹ̀* (as in ẹ̀ẹ̀kan (once).)
Identify their function in such sentences.

E What do the following nouns have in common as a result of which they are put in the same sub-class of manner nouns?

ọgán	kíákíá	ọdọọdún	júujùu
òjìjì	kìtàkìtà	méjìméjì	díẹ̀díẹ̀

CHAPTER 3

Qualifiers

3.1 Any word or grammatical (i.e. acceptable) combination of words which qualifies a noun is a **qualifier.** Thus, the word or combination of words accompanying *ìwé* (book) in each of the following four examples is a qualifier.

ìwé wúwo	(heavy book)
ìwé olùkọ́ wa	(Our teacher's book)
ìwé tí olùkọ́ wa rà	(Book that our teacher bought)
ìwé ni olùkọ́ wa rà	(It was a book that our teacher bought)

ACTUAL FUNCTION

3.2 The actual work of qualifiers is to narrow down the conceptual range or meanings of nouns. Consider the noun *ìṣu* (yam), as in:

Mo ra iṣu.　　　(I bought yams.)

This noun, as it stands in this sentence, refers to all kinds of yams—small yams, big yams, fat yams, thin yams, good yams, bad yams, white yams, yellow yams, etc. But once this same noun is qualified by a qualifier, it will no longer have the power to refer to all kinds of yams. Thus, in the following example:

Mo ra iṣu sísè.　　　(I bought cooked yam.)

it refers to the cooked variety of yams only.

DEFINITION'S IMPLICATIONS

3.3 One of the implications of the above definition is that qualifiers never occur independently in connected speech. In other words, they are not qualifiers unless they actually co-occur with and qualify something. Thus the word *wúwo*, by itself, is strictly just a word and nothing else. There is no way to tell whether it is a noun or a qualifier or a verb. But given its function in the first example above, one would have to conclude that it is, for that example, a qualifier.

Yet another implication of the same definition is that qualifiers co-occur with nouns only. For this reason, it automatically follows that any word whatsoever qualified by a qualifier is a noun. Thus, consider the following common sentence in the language:

Ṣe ni mo jókòó jẹ́ẹ́jẹ́ mi.   (I sat down without molesting anyone.)

The word *mi* (my) in the sentence is a qualifier. It qualifies *jẹ́ẹ́jẹ́* (gently). Consequently, the latter is a noun, and not an adverb as popularly believed. Some additional examples are:

Ẹ jẹ́ kí ó máa gbọ̀n rìrì rẹ̀ ní 'bẹ̀ yẹn.	(Let him/her go on trembling in *rìrì* manner there, as is his/her habit.)
Má ta félefèle rẹ dé ọ̀dọ̀ mi o.	(Now I am warning you. Don't behave in your *félefèle* manner in my presence.)
Wọ̀dùwọ̀dù wọn ni wọ́n ń ṣe lọ.	(They simply went on behaving in their usual *wọ̀dùwọ̀dù* manner.)

These examples and many others like them in the language constitute additional reason for calling all words like *rìrì*, *wọ̀dùwọ̀dù*, *félefèle*, *jẹ́ẹ́jẹ́*, *kíákíá*, *wéréwéré*, etc. nouns and not adverbs, as people wrongly believe they are, under the influence of foreign languages, most especially English. (One reason was given earlier in **2.6** and **2.18** above).

The grammatical or syntactic tie between qualifiers and the nouns they qualify is so close that they are never left behind when such nouns are 'emphasized'. This is clearly shown by the fact that the following sentence:

Mo lọ pọn omi mímu.   (I went to fetch drinking water.)

in which *mímu* is a qualifier, can properly be turned into:

Omi mímu ni mo lọ pọn.   (It was drinking water that I went to fetch.)

31

but not into:

*Omi ni mo lọ pọn mimu

in normal, acceptable Yoruba usage. ('Emphasis' is interpreted as a form of qualification in this book. See **3.16** below).

Behaviour under 'emphasis' is often a very reliable way of telling qualifiers and modifiers apart. For this, see the footnote on *nìkan* in **5.8** as well as the one on *gan-an* in **5.17** below.

MANNER OF CO-OCCURRENCE WITH NOUNS

3.4 There are some Yoruba nouns which are seldom used with qualifiers, or which are markedly restricted in the types of qualifiers they can occur with. Examples are:

kí	(What?)	òjijì	(suddenness)
ta	(Who?)	ọgán	(suddenness)
èwo	(Which one?)	òtò	(difference)
èló	(How much?)	kíákíá	(brisk manner)
mélòó[1]	(How many?)	ségesège	(no English translation)

Ó dé ti àìdé. . .   (He had scarcely arrived. . .)
(See **6.4**, **7.6** and **8.31** below).

3.5 On the other hand, there are nouns in the language which are never, or almost never, used without qualifiers.

These are:

bí/bá	(manner)	ìṣẹ́jú	(minute)
ti	(own)	èdè	(language)
gbogbo	(entirety)	oríìṣi	(variety, type)
kìkì	(alone)	ẹ̀bá	(edge)
irú	(type, variety)	èrè̀/ẹ̀ẹ̀	(time)
ìró	(sound)	òdò	(presence)
wákàtí	(hour)	ará	(folk, person)

3.6 Apart from the above two groups of nouns, all the other nouns in the language occur either accompanied or not accompanied by qualifiers, depending upon the context.

---

[1] Apparently, this word is not the same thing as the one in *mélòó kan* (a few).

3.7 Qualifiers always follow the nouns they qualify. For example:

ẹja díndín	(fried fish)
ọ̀pọ̀ ènìyàn	(a lot of people)
gbogbo ìgbà	(all times, every time)
àwọn ẹranko	(animals)

Here, *díndín, ènìyàn, ìgbà,* and *ẹranko* act as qualifiers to the nouns occurring respectively immediately to their left.

Contrary to popular belief, qualifiers are never modified by adverbs in the language. For more on this, see **6.17** below.

CLASSIFICATION

3.8 Nine different classes of qualifiers can be established in the language on the basis of their meanings, derivational origin, relation to the noun qualified, and positions of occurrence relative to one another.

3.9 Numerals

Examples:

A		**B**	
ìkan	(one)	ìkínní	(first)
méjì	(two)	ìkejì	(second)
mẹ́ta	(three)	ìkẹta	(third)
mẹ́rin	(four)	ìkẹrin	(fourth)
márùn-ún	(five)	ìkarùn-ún	(fifth)
mẹ́fà	(six)	ìkẹfà	(sixth)
méje	(seven)	ìkeje	(seventh)
méjọ	(eight)	ìkẹjọ	(eighth)
mẹ́sàn-án	(nine)	ìkẹsàn-án	(ninth)
mẹ́wàá	(ten)	ìkẹwàá	(tenth)
mọ́kànlá	(eleven)	ìkọkànlá	(eleventh)

With the possible exception of *ìkan* (one), these numerals are all derived. The ones under A are derived from nouns, while those under B are derived from phrases containing a verb followed by its object. (For more on this, see **6.7** and **6.14** below).

Yoruba words for indicating multiples of ten, e.g. *ogún* (twenty), *ọgbọ̀n* (thirty), are not in the class of numeral qualifiers. They are nouns, and can only be turned into genitival qualifiers. (See **3.15** below).

The numerals under A are traditionally known as **cardinal numerals.** They are used to indicate the exact quantity or number of the nouns they occur with. For example:

iṣu méjọ   (eight yams)

The ones under B are known as **ordinal numerals,** and are used to indicate exactly where something occurs in a series. For example:

iṣu ùkẹjọ   (the eighth yam)

The initial sound of the numerals in this group, which is very short, changes with the context; more specifically, it takes the form of the last sound of the immediately preceding noun. Examples are:

ìgi ìkínní	(the first tree)
ilé èkínní	(the first house)
kẹ̀kẹ́ ẹ̀kínní	(the first bicycle)
ajá àkínní	(the first dog)
ọjọ́ ọ̀kínní	(the first day)
oko òkínní	(the first farm)
iṣu ùkínní	(the first yam)

Cardinal and ordinal numerals cannot qualify the same noun simultaneously. Thus, in:

iṣu mẹ́wàá àkínní   (the first ten yams)

mẹ́wàá qualifies *iṣu* directly, while *ìkínní* qualifies *iṣu mẹ́wàá* rather than *iṣu* by itself.

3.10 Demonstratives

The full list of demonstratives is as follows:

ìyí/èyí	(this)	ìwọ̀nyẹn	(those)
ìyẹn	(that)	ìwo/èwo	(which?)
ìwọ̀nyí	(these)	mélòó	(how many?)

Ọmọ mélòó   (How many children?)

The initial sound of these demonstratives, with the exception

34

of *mélòó*, changes with the context: it assumes the form of the immediately preceding sound. For example:

ọmọ ọ̀nyí	(this child)	iṣẹ́ ẹ̀yí	(this piece of work)
ìwé èyí	(this book)	ajá àyí	(this dog)

3.11 Determiners

The determiners, like the demonstratives, are few in number. They consist of:

gan-an	(exact, specifically)	pàápàá	(especially)
náà	(the)	ìkan	(some, certain, a)
ṣoṣo	(single)	mélòó kan	(some, a few)
péré	(only)	káká	(sheer)
nìkan	(alone)		

agbára káká	(sheer force)
ọmọ náà	(the child)

Determiners usually (but not necessarily always) come last in strings of qualifiers attached to individual nouns.

The determiner *ṣoṣo* is used with the quantity noun *ìkan/ọ̀kan* (one) only, as in:

Ó mú ọ̀kan ṣoṣo.	(He took one only.)
Ọ̀kan ṣoṣo ni mo rí.	(I saw one only.)

The determiner *péré* occurs with quantity nouns only, as in:

Mẹ́ta péré ni mo mú.	(I took three only.)
Ọ̀kan ṣoṣo péré ni mo mú.	(I took one only.)

Notice the order in which *ṣoṣo* and *péré* co-occur.

3.12 Relative Clauses

The number of relative clauses in the language is infinite. This is because such clauses can be formed at will or as the occasion demands. They are formed from complete but simple sentences (for more on this, see **6.18—6.23** below).

Relative clauses typically begin with the introducer *tí* (see **6.18** below). For example:

tí mo rí	(that I saw)

35

tí mo ti rí i	(where I saw it)
tí wón ń pè ní Òjó	(that they call Ojo)

as in

ọmọ tí mo rí	(the child that I saw)
ibi tí mo ti rí i	(the place where I saw him)
Ọmọ tí wón ń pè ní Òjó	(the child that they call Ojo)

The introducer *tí* is invariably dropped from relative clauses qualifying the noun *bí* (manner). For example:

bí mo ti wí   (as I said)

What shows that a relative clause is present in this example is the preposition *ti,* which occurs predictably in, among other places, relative clauses of a particular kind (see **6.22** below).

The introducer *tí* can optionally be dropped from relative clauses qualifying *ẹni* (person), *ohun* (thing), *títí* (while, period), and several other nouns. For examples:

Ẹni mo rí mo bá lọ	(I went with the person I saw.)
ohun mo mú bọ̀	(what I brought back)

Dropping the introducer *tí* is actually rare, however, in standard Yoruba, though not in some of its dialects.

When qualified by relative clauses, *ìgbà* (time) is sometimes dropped in some contexts.[1] For example:

Tí ó bá dé, áá mú ìkan.	(Whenever it came, it would take one.)
léhìn tí mo ti kìlọ̀ fún ẹ	(after I have warned you)

These examples are the reduced versions, respectively, of:

Ní ìgbà tí ó bá dé, áá mú ìkan.
léhìn ìgbà tí mo ti kìlọ̀ fún ẹ

No other noun can be dropped as *ìgbà* can.

---

[1] There is no contradiction between this statement and the observation made earlier to the effect that qualifiers never occur without the nouns they qualify. In the present case, the noun *ìgbà* may be absent physically, but its meaning is always present. It is the presence of its meaning that makes it possible for people to know that it is not some other noun that has been dropped.

3.13 Adjectives

The number of adjectives in the language is quite large. The vast majority, if not all, of such adjectives are derived. They are derived from nouns and verb phrases in relative clauses (see **6.18** below). For example:

rere	(good (character)).	díẹ̀	(few)
dúdú	(black)	mímu	(drinking)
funfun	(white)	sísè	(cooked)
gbogbo	(every)	gbígbìn	(for planting)
púpọ̀	(many)		

ọmọ rere (good child)	ẹran sísè (cooked meat)
ọjọ́ gbogbo (every day)	oúnjẹ díẹ̀ (some food)
omi mímu (drinking water)	

3.14 Appositive Qualifiers

This class of qualifiers is quite large. The members of the class are all derived from nouns with or without their own qualifiers in relative clauses (see **6.18** below). Examples are

ènìyàn	(people)	tálákà	(poor)
ọdẹ	(hunter)	ọkùnrin	(man)
sójà	(soldier)	obìnrin	(woman)
àpèkánukò	(pronounced with rounded lips)		

ọmọkùnrin (= ọmọ ọkùnrin)	(male child, boy)
owó àpèkánukò	(money, pronounced with round lips)
ògbójú ọdẹ	(brave hunter)

Words in this class are traditionally known as nouns, and are said to be in apposition to the nouns they accompany. Actually, however, such words are qualifiers, because their relation to the nouns they occur with is exactly the same as the one between adjectives, for instance, and the nouns they qualify. Thus, in:

Sídí, ìyàwó mi   (Sídí, my wife)

the appositive qualifier *ìyàwó mi* narrows down the range of people that *Sídí* could refer to.

37

An appositive qualifier and the noun it qualifies always refer to the same thing. For this reason, it is always possible to drop the noun qualified without any significant loss of meaning. Thus, these two sentences mean practically the same thing:

Sídí, ìyàwó mi ti dé.   (My wife, Sídí, has returned.)
Ìyàwó mi ti dé.   (My wife has returned.)

In this last sentence, however, *ìyàwó mi* is no longer a qualifier. It has become a subject noun accompanied by its qualifier *mi* (my).

3.15 Genitival Qualifiers

The number of items in this class is extremely large. In fact, for all practical purposes, it is infinite. All the items in the class are nouns with or without their own qualifiers that have been made to function as qualifiers. For example:

ènìyàn	(people)	Èkó	(Lagos)
ẹranko	(animal)	kí	(what?)
igi	(tree, wood)	àná	(yesterday)
ilé	(house)	ta	(who?)
Dàda	(Dada)	èló	(how much?)

ọmọ ènìyàn	(human offspring)
ọba Èkó	(the king of Lagos)
ìyàwó Dàda	(Dàda's wife)
ìrọ̀lẹ́ àná	(yesterday evening, last night)
ilé ta ni?	(whose house is it?)

Qualifiers like these are mostly derived from nouns with or without their own qualifiers in relative clauses. Such qualifiers are used to express a wide range of concepts. Some examples are:

   i. OWNERSHIP

ìyàwó Dàda	(Dada's wife)
owó Dàda	(Dada's money)

   ii. ORIGIN

ọmọ Ọ̀yọ́	(child from Ọyọ)
ará ibí	(native of this place)

38

àpò owó	(bag in which money is kept)
ọ̀bẹ ẹran	(knife for butchering animals)

Which of these and other similar concepts a particular example expresses depends to a great extent upon the relative clause from which the example itself was derived. Thus,

owó Dàda   (Dada's money)

expresses the concept of ownership, among other things, because the phrase ordinarily means the same thing as:

owó tí Dàda ní   (the money that Dada has)

Similarly, the phrase

ọ̀bẹ ẹran   (butchering knife)

expresses purpose, as it has the same meaning as

ọ̀bẹ tí wọn fi ń kun ẹran   (the knife that people use for butchering animals)

Most items in the language each have the same form whether they are functioning as nouns or as genitival qualifiers. The polymorphic nouns are an exception. They have special forms that they assume when functioning as genitival qualifiers. The forms are

ìmi	(my)	iwa	(our)
ìrẹ	(your)	iyín	(your) *(pl.)*.
irè	(his, her, its)	iwọn	(their)

These forms cannot all occur freely with every noun in the language, for different reasons. A few of the nouns that some of these qualifiers cannot occur freely with are

ti	(own)	kìkì	(only)
bí	(manner)	gbogbo	(entirety)

The sound at the beginning of these genitival qualifiers changes with the context: it assumes the same form as the last sound of the immediately preceding word. For example

igi ìrẹ	(your tree, stick)	ọwọ́ ọ̀rẹ	(your hand)
ìwé èrẹ	(your book)	owó òrẹ	(your money)
ọ̀rẹ́ ẹ̀rẹ	(your friend)	ojú ùrẹ	(your face/eyes)
ọ̀gá àrẹ	(your master)		

When a genitival qualifier begins with a consonantal sound (see Chapter 9), the last sound of the noun immediately preceding the qualifier is automatically 'lengthened' on a mid-tone (but see Section **10.24** below). For example

owóo Dàda	(Dada's money)
ẹsẹ̀ẹ̀ Dàda	(Dada's foot)
okoo Dàda	(Dada's farm)
títí i Sátídé	(by Saturday)
gbogboo sójà	(all soldiers)

This kind of lengthening normally does not occur when appositive qualifiers are involved.[1] For this reason, it is sometimes useful for telling appositive and genitival constructions apart. Other, more reliable ways of telling these two constructions apart exist, however. One such way involves meaning: the two constructions convey different kinds of meanings.

Meaning also provides a ready means of differentiating these two constructions from a third type of construction exemplified by:

méjì tọ́rọ́ (two for three kobo)

There is no qualifier present in this latter construction. The two words there are nouns. The second noun always comes from the class of Value Nouns, and the first from the class of Quantity Nouns.

3.16 Topical Qualifiers
The number of items in this class is infinite. This is because members of the class can be created at will. They are always created from sentences, and are always easily recognizable by the introducer *ni* which occurs at their beginning. Examples are

ni mo rà	(what I bought)
ni ó rà ìwé	(that bought books)
ni mo ra ìwé	(that I bought books)

---

[1] One possible exception to this observation is *ilée ti irẹ̀* (his own house) where the noun *ti* plus its qualifier seems to function as appositive qualifier to *ilé*.

ìwé ni mo rà	(Books are what I bought.)
èmi ni ó ra ìwé	(I am the person that bought books.)
rírà ni mo ra ìwé	(The fact is that I bought books.)

In these examples, *ìwé, èmi,* and *rírà* are qualified by the topical qualifiers attached to them. The relation between these nouns and the qualifiers attached to them is essentially the same as the one between any noun and any other type of qualifier already exemplified.

To begin with, a topical qualifier follows the noun it qualifies, exactly as other qualifiers do.

Furthermore, a topical qualifier, like other qualifiers, narrows down the potential field of choice to just the item qualified. Put another way, it reduces the list of items out of which a choice is to be made to only one item, namely, the one which the topical qualifier itself accompanies. Thus, in the first example: *ìwé,* is segregated from all the other things that 'I' could conceivably have bought, such as *bàtà, èwù, ọkọ̀,* etc. Topical qualifiers, like other qualifiers, cannot occur with the polymorphic nouns (see **2.21** above).

A noun can be qualified by a string of two or more topical qualifiers, just as it can be qualified by two or more relative clauses (see **8.31** below). ...

Topical qualifiers and relative clauses are interchangeable in some contexts (see **6.26** and **8.31** below.)

Finally, relative clauses and topical qualifiers are formed in exactly the same way (see **6.25** below). Not only that, for almost (but not all) every noun plus topical qualifier construction in the language, there is a corresponding noun plus relative clause construction.

All these similarities simply cannot be accidental; hence the decision in this book to put relative clauses and topical qualifiers in the same class, *viz.* of qualifiers.

However, one important difference exists between topical qualifiers and other kinds of qualifiers. Any noun qualified by any of the other kinds of qualifiers is normally employed like that only as subject or object. A noun qualified by a topical qualifier, on the other hand, can be employed either as a sentence or as an object noun phrase. Thus, the objects of the verbs *ṣe* 'to be' and *mọ̀* 'to know' in the following two sentences consist of nouns qualified by topical qualifiers.

Kì í ṣe ìwé ni mo rà.   (A book wasn't what I bought.)
N kò mọ kí ni ó fà á.   (I don't know the reason for it.)

For a discussion of sentences consisting only of nouns and their topical qualifiers, see **8.31** below.

3.17 Interrogative Qualifiers

This class consists of five qualifiers that are used for asking questions. The qualifiers are:

ta	(who?)	èló	(how much?)
kí	(what?)	mélòó	(how many?)
èwo	(which one?)		

Ìwé ta ni ìyẹn?	(Whose book is that?)
Owó kí ni o fẹ́?	(What do you want money for?)
Ọmọ wo ni ó bú ẹ?	(Which boy insulted you?)
Iṣu èló ni o ra?	(How much yam did you buy?)
Ọmọ mélòó ni ó wá?	(How many children were present?)

The initial sound of one of these qualifiers, *viz. èwo*, changes with the context.

CO-OCCURRENCE OF QUALIFIERS

3.18 A noun can have a string of two or more qualifiers attached to itself. For example:

Ọkọ̀ ayọ́kẹ́lẹ́ dúdú mẹ́ta tí   (They damaged the three black
mo rà ni wọ́n bàjẹ́.   cars that I bought.)

In this sentence:

ọkọ̀	is the noun qualified.
ayọ́kẹ́lẹ́	is an appositive qualifier.
dúdú	is an adjective.
mẹ́ta	is a numeral.
tí mo rà	is a relative clause.
ni wọ́n bàjẹ́	is a topical qualifier.

3.19 The order in which qualifiers occur with themselves is partially free and partially fixed. This topic is beyond the scope of the present book. It will be treated in detail elsewhere.

COMPREHENSION

1. What do qualifiers do?
2. Are qualifiers always single words?
3. What do qualifiers occur with? Can they also occur by themselves?
4. What effect do qualifiers have on the meanings of the nouns they qualify?
5. What nouns are seldom used with qualifiers?
6. What nouns cannot be used without qualifiers?
7. What nouns can be used with or without qualifiers?
8. How do qualifiers always occur in relation to the nouns that they qualify?
9. How many sub-classes of qualifiers are set up in this chapter? On what bases were they set up?
10. How many kinds of numerals are there? How do they differ from each other?
11. What are numerals derived from?
12. What is the identifying or distinguishing feature of relative clauses?
13. What are most adjectives derived from?
14. What are appositive qualifiers?
15. What are genitival qualifiers and how do they differ from appositive qualifiers?
16. What is the distinguishing feature of topical qualifiers?
17. How do topical qualifiers differ from other qualifiers?
18. What are interrogative qualifiers?

EXERCISES

A Two ways have now been suggested of recognizing nouns in Yoruba—one in Chapter 2 and another in the present chapter. What are they? Use either or both of them to prove that the following words function as nouns in the language. Offer a separate proof for each word.

kí	(what?)
ta	(who?)
ti	(that of) (as in *ti òjó*)
bí	(manner, like) (as in *bí òṣùpá*)
gbogbo	(all, entirety)

43

kìkì	(alone)
ṣàṣà	(few)
èrè/èè	(time) (as in *èè kan* 'once')
títí	(period duration, until)
gégé	(exactly)
àwọn	(plural entities) (as in *àwọn èdá*)

Which is the more preferable of the two ways of recognizing nouns? Why do you think that it is?

B What is said about qualifiers in this chapter suggests that three more sub-classes of nouns could be set up in addition to those set up in Chapter 2. What are these three additional sub-classes? Why do you think they were not mentioned in Chapter 2?

C In Section **3.18** it is stated that a noun can be qualified by a series of qualifiers. Such qualifiers will have to occur one after another, to the right of the particular noun they qualify. Determine the order of co-occurrence of such qualifiers. (*Note* that you cannot do this until you have studied many sentences like the example in Section **3.18**).

D On the basis of what you have discovered for yourself under Exercise **C**, do you find the statement made in Section **3.19** true or false? If false, suggest a more accurate formulation.

E Show how the important statement about qualifiers made in Section **3.7** follows from the discussion of nouns in Chapter 2.

F Here is a definition of Yoruba qualifiers.

> 'If a word tells us more about the meaning of a noun (or pronoun) so as to show its quality or the distinction between the noun and other nouns, the word is an adjective.'

Compare this definition with the one offered in the present chapter, clearly bringing out the differences and similarities (if any) between them.

CHAPTER 4

Verbs

4.1 Any word functioning as predicator in a grammatical or acceptable sentence in the language is a **verb**.

ACTUAL FUNCTION

4.2 Predicator is a highly technical term in modern grammar. As used here, it refers to the position between the subject and object in the following sentences:

SUBJECT	PREDICATOR	OBJECT	
Mo	ra	işu	(I bought yams.)
Iná	jó	ilé	(Fire burned houses.)
Qba	pa	àşe	(The king gave an order.)

In the next set of sentences, predicator comes directly after subject: the sentences have no objects.

SUBJECT	PREDICATOR	
Òjó	sùn	(Ojo slept.)
Ó	dára	(It is good.)
Ó	dúdú	(It is black.)
Òun	dà	(Where is it?)

All these examples are grammatical sentences in the language. Each of the words appearing there under predicator functions as predicator. For this reason, each such word is a verb.

DEFINITION'S IMPLICATIONS

4.3 The above definition is based on the traditional assumption that verbs occur at the rate of one per simple sentence. Only one verb occurs in each of the seven examples above, and this makes them simple sentences.

45

If a sentence containing just one verb is a simple sentence, then one containing two or more verbs is not a simple sentence; it is a complex sentence. From the standpoint of the above definition, complex sentences are formed by combining appropriate parts of simple sentences. This implies that if any sentence is truly complex, then it must be possible to break it down into the simple sentences that were combined to form it. Thus, the sentence

Mo ra ẹran jẹ.   (I bought meat and ate it.)

is complex, because it contains more than one verb. Specifically, it contains the verbs *rà* (buy) and *jẹ* (eat). It was actually formed by combining the following two simple sentences:

Mo ra ẹran.   (I bought meat.)
Mo jẹ ẹran.   (I ate meat.)

We know this because these two simple sentences combined mean much the same thing as the corresponding complex sentence above.

The following sentence, too, is complex.

Ọkọ̀ tí o rà dà?   (Where is the vehicle you bought?)

It contains two verbs, *rà* (buy) and *dà* (where is?). It has the same meaning as the following two simple sentences combined:

Ọkọ̀ dà?   (Where is (the) vehicle?)
O ra ọkọ̀.   (You bought a vehicle.)

In other words, the complex sentence above was formed by combining these two simple sentences.

In general, the number of verbs contained in any complex sentence is the same as the number of simple sentences that were combined to form the complex sentence itself. Thus, if a complex sentence contains two verbs, it will be the case that it was formed by combining at least two simple sentences.

We have so far been discussing truly complex sentences. The term 'truly complex sentences' carries with it the suggestion or implication that there are sentences which appear to be complex but which are in fact not complex. One such sentence is:

Ó ba ilé náà jẹ́.   (It damaged the building.)

46

This sentence appears to contain two verbs, *bà* and *jẹ́*. But the sentence cannot be broken down into two simple sentences. This is shown by the fact that the following two simple sentences, which one would have thought were combined to form the above sentence, do not mean the same thing as the sentence itself.

      *Ó ba ilé náà.
      *Ó jẹ́ ilé náà.

Indeed, these two simple sentences are meaningless in the present context.

From the standpoint of the above definition of verbs, seemingly complex sentences which in fact cannot be broken down into grammatical simple sentences are actually not complex. Rather they are simple, and therefore actually each contain one verb, which may or may not be accompanied by modifiers. (For modifiers, see Chapter 5.)

4.4 Speakers know what are verbs in the language. Although they appear to do so by instinct, the real explanation, in fact, is that, right from infancy, they have learnt to associate a particular place or position in Yoruba sentences with verbs and with verbs only. That position is the one labelled predicator above.

It is because of this association that they know when something is being 'used as a verb'. For example, in

Ó wàhálà mi púpọ̀.   (He bothered me a great deal.)
Ẹ pàtàkì ara yín.   (Make yourself feel important.)

where 'the nouns *wàhálà* (troubles) and *pàtàkì* (importance) are used as verbs'.

It is for this same reason that they know what are verbs even in sentences they may never have heard before. For example:

Wọ́n 'vónò' yàrá méjì.   (They 'vonoed' two rooms.)
Wọ́n 'ọ̀ọ̀pù' owó kòkó.   (They 'upped' the price of cocoa beans.)

These two sentences have probably never been spoken before in the language. Yet, no mature speaker who has been assured that the sentences are grammatical would be in doubt as to the verbs there.

47

4.5 The only way to form new verbs in the language is to make words which are otherwise not verbs in Yoruba function as predicator. That is the way the verbs *wàhálà* (to bother someone), *pàtàkì* (to make oneself feel important) in the examples given earlier, and *gàdrí* (to cater for) and *gẹlẹtẹ* (to stay idle) in the following examples, entered the language.

Ta ni ó ń gààrí rẹ?	(Who is taking care of all your needs?)
Olówó gẹlẹtẹ, ìwòfà gẹlẹtẹ.	(The servant stays idle, exactly as his master does.)

SUBJECT SELECTION

4.6 Every verb can be used with a noun functioning as its subject. For example:

Ìwọ dà?	(May I see you for a minute?)
Ó tó.	(That's enough!)
Ó tì.	(That's not possible. No!)
Ilẹ̀ gbẹ.	(The ground is dry.)

However, invariably because of its meaning, every verb has a list (whether long or short) of nouns that alone can function as its subject. Thus, *wà* means (to be (in a place)). And since everything has to be in some place or another, one finds that almost any noun can function as the verb's subject. For example:

Oúnjẹ wà.	(Food is available (for sale).)
Ọ̀rọ̀ wà.	(We have things to talk about.)

The list of nouns that can function as the subject of *mọ̀* (know), on the other hand, is not as long as that of nouns that can function as the subject of *wà*. The nouns that function as the subject of *mọ̀* always represent beings or things that can think or are assumed to be able to think. For example:

Mo mọ̀.	(I know.)
Obìnrin náà mọ̀.	(The woman knows.)

In contrast to *mọ̀* and especially *wà*, only a few nouns can function under normal circumstances as the subject of *rọ̀* (to rain) and *yé* (to lay (eggs)). For example:

Òjò rọ̀ ní àná.	(It rained yesterday.)
Adìẹ náà yé ẹyin mẹ́fà.	(The hen laid six eggs.)

48

4.7 A syllable having a high-tone and the same quality as the last sound of the subject automatically occurs, with some exceptions, between the subject and the verb. For example:

Ilẹ̀ ẹ́ gbẹ.   (The ground is/was dry.)

There has long been uncertainty among grammarians as to the precise form and function of the syllable. It seems very doubtful whether a perfect solution will ever be found to this problem. The position taken in the present book is that, all things considered, the syllable is best analysed as a pre-verbal adverb for indicating past/present action. (For Pre-verbal Adverbs, see **5.8** below).

In this connection, notice first of all that the syllable occurs between the Subject and the Predicator, the very place where some adverbs occur in the language. For instance, this is where the adverbs for indicating future action occur; that is, the adverbs *yóò, óò,· á,* and *máa.* The fact that the syllable occurs where adverbs occur is an indication that it is itself an adverb.

Secondly, with only one exception (see **5.11** below), every Yoruba sentence in which the syllable in question occurs refers to past/present action. For example:

Ilẹ̀ ẹ́ gbẹ.   (The ground is/was dry.)
Ayọ̀ ọ́ lọ.   (Ayọ went.)

Conversely, sentences in which the syllable does not occur in any shape or form (see **5.11** below), never refer to past/present action; instead, they always refer to future action. For example:

Ilẹ̀ á gbẹ.   (The ground will be dry.)
Ayọ̀ óò lọ.   (Ayọ will go.)

The syllable's manner of occurrence as shown by these examples strongly suggests that the syllable itself is in fact the element which signifies past/present action in Yoruba sentences.

Now, if the syllable signifies past/present action, as claimed, and if the adverbs *yóò, óò, á,* and *máa* for their part signify future action, then any Yoruba sentence which contains neither the syllable nor any one of the adverbs *yóò, óò, á,* and *máa* should not refer to any particular time. In other words, such a sentence should be timeless, in the sense of not referring specifically to either past time or present time or future time. This is in fact the case, as the following sentences show.

Èjì dín l'ógún	(lit. two minus twenty, i.e. 'eighteen')
Òjì l'úgba	(lit. forty plus two-hundred i.e. 'two hundred and forty')
Wèrèpè gba 'ra rẹ̀ gba 'gi oko.	(The cow-itch protects the tree supporting it in the process of protecting its own self.)
Ẹ̀wọ̀n já ní 'bi ó wù ú.	(The chain breaks just where it pleases.)

The syllable under discussion is completely absent from each of the above sentences. Similarly for the adverbs *yóò, óò, á,* and *máa*. The actions signified in the sentences are not located in any specific time, neither in the past, nor in the present, nor in the future. Such sentences, therefore, further confirm the view that the syllable being discussed is the actual element signifying past/present action in Yoruba.

The high-tone syllable here re-analysed as a pre-verbal adverb changes its form with the context. Since that particular kind of change of form is ordinarily possible in the language only with the vowel *i*, the basic or true form of the syllable or adverb will be represented as *í*. For more on it, see **5.11** below.

OBJECT SELECTION

4.8 With the exception of *dà* (where is?) and *ńkọ́* (where is?) every verb can be used with an object. For example:

Ó ra kẹ̀kẹ́.	(He bought a bicycle.)
Ó kọ́ ilé.	(He built a house.)
Ayọ̀ kò lọ lílọ kànkan.	(Ayọ didn't go at all.)
Mo lá àlá.	(I dreamt.)

In these examples, *kẹ̀kẹ́* (bicycle), *ilé* (house), *lílọ kànkan* (any kind of going), and *àlá* (a dream) function as the objects of the verbs in their respective sentences.

Notice that the third sentence above contains the verb *lọ* (to go). That verb and many others like it are traditionally referred to in Yoruba grammar as intransitive verbs, i.e. verbs which never take or occur with objects. With the exception of the two verbs mentioned earlier, all the members of the traditional class of intransitive verbs are here analysed as transitive, i.e. as capable of taking objects. That such verbs are in fact transitive, contrary to popular belief, can be seen most clearly in the case of those of them having a low tone. It is a rule of Yoruba grammar that when an object follows a monosyllabic verb with low tone, that tone becomes mid tone (see **4.10** below). This tone change regularly occurs in the case of the so-called intransitive verbs with low tone, as in:

dùn	: Ó dun dídùn oyin.	(It tastes sweet like honey.)
rọ̀	: Ó rọ rírọ̀ ẹ̀kọ.	(It feels soft like ẹkọ.)

(For more on sentences like these, see **8.26** below).
For this reason, there is no syntactic need to recognize a class of intransitive verbs as distinct from transitive verbs in the language. This book will therefore not talk of verbs being transitive or intransitive, but rather of their taking or not taking objects, depending upon the context.

Some verbs are always used with objects. Examples are:

lá	(to dream)	gún	(to pound, to stab)
kọ	(to sing)	ro	(to weed (with a hoe))
lé	(to chase off, to pursue)	kà	(to read)

Other verbs are used with or without object, as context demands. Examples are:

lọ	(to go)	jẹ	(to eat)
wà	(to be (in a place))	mu	(to drink)
bí	(to give birth)	kéré	(be small)
sùn	(to sleep)	gbọ́n	(be wise)
sá	(to run)	gọ̀	(be foolish)

4.9 Because of their meanings, verbs vary in their ability to take objects. Some verbs can take an infinitely large number of nouns as object. For example: *mọ̀* (to know):

Ó mọ iṣẹ́.	(He is skilful.)
Ó mọ Èkó.	(He knows Lagos.)
Ó mọ Dàda.	(He knows Dada.)
Kò mọ há.	(He doesn't know a thing.)

Others can take only a small number of nouns as object. For example, kọ́ (to build) which can take only the following nouns referring to places of dwelling as object.

ilé	(house)	ahéré	(hut)
pẹ̀tẹ́ẹ̀sì	(a storey house)	mọ́ṣáláṣí	(mosque)
abà	(hut)	ṣọ́ọ̀ṣì	(church)

(Notice that this list excludes àgọ́ (hut, tent) and ihò (hole).) Still other verbs with highly specific meanings each occur with only one noun as object.   Examples are:

lá (àlá)	(to dream)	gbọ́n (ọgbọ́n)	(be wise)
kọ (orin)	(to sing)	gọ̀ (agọ̀)	(be foolish)
jó (ijó)	(to dance)	pa (àdé)	(to meet)
kò (iná)	(to poke fire)		

4.10 The low-tone of monosyllabic verbs becomes mid-tone before objects other than those from the polymorphic class. For example:

mò:	Mo mọ ilé rẹ̀.	(I know his residence.)
kò:	Ó kọ oúnjẹ.	(He refused to eat.)
wò:	Ó wọ ẹ̀wọ̀n.	(He went to prison.)

This change in tone is often the only indication that a particular noun is or is not functioning as the object of a verb.   For example:

Mo mò kíákíá.	(I knew quickly.)
Mo mọ kíákíá.	(I know (the word) kíákíá.)
Mo gbà pé kí ó lọ.	(I agree that he should go.)
Mo gba pé kí ó lọ.	(What I'll accept is that he should go.)

In any sentence where the low tone of the verb does not change, the noun or nominalisation directly following such a verb is the object of a suppressed preposition, namely ní (in, on, at). (More on this in **5.21** and **5.30** below). For additional examples of sentences like the above, see **4.19**, and **9.10** below.

52

CLASSIFICATION

4.11 Key sentence constructions in the language are distinguished from one another primarily by the types of verbs operating in them. For this reason, verbs are subdivisible into several classes on the basis of which of such constructions they can operate in. Verbs which can operate in more than one such construction correspondingly belong in more than one class. In other words, if a particular verb can operate in three different key sentence constructions, then it is a member of three distinct classes of verbs.

4.12 Serial Verbs

These verbs get their name from the way they occur in strings or series of two or more per sentence. Their class is made up of almost all the verbs in the language. E.g.:

rà	(buy)	mọ́	(to stick onto)
pa	(kill)	sè	(cook)
jẹ	(eat)	tà	(sell)
tì	(be impossible)		

Ó ra ẹran jẹ. (He bought meat and ate it.)
Ó ṣe é tì.)
Ó tì í ṣe.) (He couldn't do it.)
Ó se ẹran tà. (He cooked meat for sale.)

For more on Serial Verbs, see **8.16** and **8.17** below.

4.13 Splitting Verbs

When used with an object, each verb in this class is always split into two halves, and the object is inserted between them. This is where the verbs in the class got their name from. Many of them have idiomatic meanings. Examples are:

bàjẹ́	(damage, spoil)
báwí	(to scold, rebuke)
réjẹ	(to cheat, swindle)
túnsè	(to recook)
gbàgbọ́	(to believe)
bẹ̀wò	(to visit)
tànjẹ	(to deceive)

53

yípo	(to surround)
padà	(turn over, turn round)
papò	(to combine)
bámu	(to match, fit well)
túká	(to disperse, scatter)
bàtì	(fail to accomplish)
bùkù	(to disparage)
bùṣe	(be almost completed)
jẹgún	(to embezzle with impunity)
patì	(to set aside)
padé	(to close, shut)
dìmú	(to grip, hold)
dání	(to hold)

Kinní kan ba Òjó jẹ́.	(Ojo has a weakness.)
Ọlọ́pàá tú wọn ká.	(The police dispersed them.)
Òjó tàn mí jẹ.	(Ojo deceived me.)
Ó tún ẹran náà sè.	(She re-cooked the meat.)
Mo gbà ẹ́ gbọ́.	(I believe you.)

For more on Splitting Verbs, see **8.17** below.

4.14 Echoing Verbs

There are only a few verbs in this class. Each of them occurs twice per sentence. The second occurrence could loosely be said to echo the first. Hence the name suggested for the verbs. They are:

fẹ́	(want)	mò	(to know)
kù	(remain)	rò	(to think)
bí	(give birth to)	ṣe	(to affect)
dá	(leave, let go)		

Ayé ò fẹ́'ni fẹ́ ọrọ̀.	(The world is never happy to see one prosper.)
Ìwọ l'ó kù mí kù.	(You are the only person I've got now.)
Ìwà à-bí-'ni-bí.	(An inherited behaviour.)
Má dá mi dá iṣẹ́ náà.	(Don't leave me alone to do the work.)

Sídí ni wón mò mí mò.   (Sidi is the only girl people see me
                              with.)
Rò mí ro 're.   (You should wish me well.)
Má jé kí ó şe mi şe é.   (You had better not provoke me.)

For more on Echoing Verbs, see **8.18** below.

4.15 Complex Verbs

Complex verbs are complex in form. In meaning, such verbs
are like simple verbs such as *rí* (see), *wá* (come), etc. But
when they are used in sentences, they behave exactly like
combinations of verbs and their objects.   Examples are:

gbàgbé	(to forget)
rántí	(to remember)
şíwó	(to stop (doing something)
dààmú	(to worry, be worried)
wàhálà	(to bother)
dúńbú	(to slaughter)
kojá	(to pass by, to exceed)
pèlú	(to accompany, to be added to)
fòòró	(to subject to stress)
jéwó	(to confess, admit guilt)
kiri	(to cover an area walking, riding, etc., to hawk wares)
gelètè	(to be idle, unoccupied)
bèrè	(to begin, to start)
bèrè	(to ask)
şubú	(to fall down)
jókòó	(to sit down)

Àwon olópàá wàhálà Òjó.   (The police gave Ojo a hard
                              time.)
Wón wàhálà rè.   (They gave him a hard time.)
Mo rántí ìre.   (I remember you.)

Many of the verbs in this class, like those in the class of splitting verbs, have idiomatic meanings. Sometimes it is on the
basis of such idiomatic meanings alone that one can differentiate between them and ordinary combinations of verbs and
object nouns. For example:

ṣíwọ́	(to stop doing something)	ṣíwọ́ (ṣí ọwọ́)	(to remove one's hands)
lajú	(be sophisticated)	lajú (la ojú)	(to open one's eyes)
lawọ́	(to·be generous)	lawọ́ (la ọwọ́)	(to open one's clenched fists)
fasẹ̀	(to be slowed down)	fasẹ̀ (fa ẹsẹ̀)	(pull legs/feet)
gbésẹ̀	(to be deceased) ·	gbésẹ̀ (gbé ẹsẹ̀)	(move one's leg/feet)
yíwọ́	(to get out of hand)	yíwọ́ (yí ọwọ́)	(to turn the hands of)

New verbs, particularly if they are more than one syllable long, are always put in this class. E.g.:

gààrí	(to cater for)
wáànì	(to crank up an·engine, to wind)
písíìsì	(to take down to pieces (e.g. of a car engine))
bíréèkì	(to apply the brakes)
ṣọ́ọ̀kì	(to chock)
kéré	(to lower the stature or esteem of)

Ṣé o ti ṣọ́ọ̀kì ọkọ̀ náà?	(Have you chocked the wheel of the vehicle?)
Bẹ́ẹ̀ ni, mo ti ṣọ́ọ̀kì irẹ̀.	(Yes, I have.)
Irú nǹkan bẹ́ẹ̀ a máa kéré ènìyàn.	(Such things tend to lower one's esteem or prestige.)

4.16 Adjectivisable Verbs

Adjectives can be formed from many, but not all, verb phrases in the language. Verb phrases from which adjectives can be formed as in the examples below, contain verbs belonging in the class of adjectivisable verbs. Examples of such verbs are:

dúdú	(to be black)	gan	(to be stiff, frozen hard)
ga	(to be tall)	wú	(to swell)
kúrú	(to be short)	kún	(to be full)
kéré	(to be small)	rún	(to crumble)
dára	(to be good)		

Aṣọ náà dúdú.	(The cloth is black.) ·
Aṣọ dúdú	(Black cloth)
Igi yìí ga.	(This tree is tall.)
Igi gíga yìí	(This tall tree)

Ẹja náà rún wómúwómú.　(The dried fish was crushed
　　　　　　　　　　　　　　　into tiny bits)
ẹja rírún　　　　　　　　　(crushed up dried fish)

For the formation of Adjectives, see **6.16** and **6.17** below.

4.17　Nominal Assimilating Verbs

The construction in which the verbs in this class function
always contains adverbial phrases where the preposition *ní*
is followed directly by nominalisations of the C_1 íC_1—type;
i.e. nominalisations like *lílọ* (going), *fífi-kọ-ìwé* (writing with).
In the construction, the preposition *ní* and the initial sounds
of the nominalisations following it can be dropped optionally.
When that happens, the new initial sounds of the nominalisations take on the same form as the final sounds of any immediately preceding words. Such immediately preceding words
are either the nominal assimilating-verbs or their objects.
Examples of the verbs in the class are:

dùn	(be pleasant)	kọ́	(to learn)
ṣòro	(be difficult)	mọ̀	(to know)
ṣe	(be possible)	wù	(to please)
ní	(to have)	pẹ́	(to be late)
yé	(to stop)	fẹ́rẹ̀	(be almost, not heavy)
fẹ́	(to want)		

Ó fẹ́ 'ílọ.)
Ó fẹ́ 'élọ.)　　　　　　　(He wants to go.)
Ó dùn ní jíjẹ.)
Ọ dùn 'únjẹ.)　　　　　　(It tastes good.)
Ó mọ ọkọ̀ ní wíwà.)
Ó mọ ọkọ̀ 'ọ́wà.)　　　　(He can drive.)
Kò yé ariwo ní pípa.)
Kò yé ariwo 'ópa.)　　　(He refuses to stop making noise.)

For more on nominal assimilating-verbs, see **8.19** below.

4.18　Particle-Selecting Verbs

The verbs in this class occur in a construction which features
the particle *ní*. This particle has no concrete meaning, and

it is completely distinct from each of the five other words spelt and pronounced as *ní* in the language (see **6.40**). The verbs in the particle-selecting class are fairly numerous. Examples are:

jí	(to steal)	rántí	(to remind)
wá	(to look for)	ṣe	(to do, hurt)
pè	(to call)	jó	(to burn)
gún	(to stab)	jẹ	(to affect)
rán	(to send)	wò	(to look at)

Òjó rán mi ní etí.	(Ojo reminded me.)
Ẹranko náà ṣe é ní èṣe.	(The animal injured him.)
Wò mí ní ojú!	(Look at my face!)
Wọ́n pè mí ní ọ̀lẹ.	(They called me a lazy drone.)

For more on Particle-Selecting Verbs, see **8.20** below.

4.19 Report Verbs

These are the verbs used for reporting or quoting thoughts, observations, orders, wishes, and requests. Some of the verbs in the class are:

ní	(to say that)	gbàgbọ́	(to believe)
sọ	(to say)	gbàgbé	(to forget)
wí	(to say)	mọ̀	(to know)
gbọ́	(to hear)	fẹ́	(to want)
lérí	(to vow)	rò	(to think)
jẹ́	(to permit, allow)	rántí	(to remember)

The nominalisations introduced by *pé, kí,* etc., following these verbs in the following examples, function in adverbial phrases whose preposition *ní* has been dropped.

Ó ní (pé) òun kò níí wá.	(He said he would not come.)
Mo gbọ́ pé o dé l'ánàá.	(I learned that you returned yesterday.)
Mo fẹ́ kí o tètè dé.	(I want you to return in time.)
Òjò kò jẹ́ kí n wá.	(Rain prevented me from coming.)

That the nominalisations following such verbs function as part of adverbial phrases is shown in part by the fact that they often can be replaced by *bẹ́ẹ̀* (so), as in:

Mo gbọ́ bẹ́ẹ̀.   (So I heard.)

Notice that the adverbial *ní méjìméjì* is replaced in precisely the same way in:

Wọ́n lọ ní méjìméjì.   (They went there in pairs.)

Wọ́n lọ bẹ́ẹ̀.   (They went there like that/in that manner.)

It is also shown in part by the well-known fact that (report) verbs with low tone never change this low tone to mid tone before such nominalisations. For example:

Ó gbà pé kí Òjó lọ.   (He agrees that Ojo should go.)

If such nominalisations were not functioning as part of adverbial phrases, the low tone of any verbs preceding them would automatically be changed to mid tone (see **4.10** above). For example:

Ó gba pé kí Òjó lọ.   (It requires that Ojo go.)

Here, the nominalisation *pé kí Òjó lọ* functions as the object of the verb *gbà*, as indicated by the change in the latter's tone.

It is reported (by informants) that in Lagos, some people say:

Mo gbọ́ ní pe ní o lọ.   (I learnt that you went.)

which definitely displays the preposition *ní*. Cf.

Mo gbọ́ pe ní o lọ.   (I learnt that you went.)

in the Oṣogbo dialect (according to informants.)

For more on Report Verbs, see **8.21** below.

4.20 Impersonal Verbs

The verbs in this class are called impersonal verbs for the simple reason that they occur in a type of sentence whose subject, ó, never refers to anybody or anything in particular. Some of the verbs are:

yẹ	(to be fitting)	dájú	(to be without doubt)
burú	(to be bad)	hàn	(to appear)
pẹ́	(to be late)	dára	(to be good)
tọ́	(to be morally right)	wù	(to please, appeal to)
kù	(to remain)		

59

Ó yẹ kí o lọ.	(You ought to go there.)
Ó pẹ́ kí Òjó tó 'ódé.	(It was a long time before Ojo returned.)
Ó kù kí á lọ mu ọtí.	(The only thing left now is for us to go and drink.)
Ó dára pé o tètè dé.	(It is good that you returned in good time.)

The nominalisations introduced by *kí* and *pé,* following impersonal verbs in the above sentences function in adverbial phrases whose preposition *ní* has been dropped. This is why the first sentence, for example, can be reduced to:

Ó yẹ bẹ́ẹ̀. (It is fitting like that.)

(Cf. **4.19** above).

It is reported (by informants) that in Lagos, some people say:

Ó yẹ ní kí o lọ. (You ought to go.)

in which the item *ní* may in fact be the preposition *ní* that is dropped in standard Yoruba. See **4.19** above, for another similar example from the Lagos dialect, and **8.22** for more on impersonal verbs.

4.21 Causative Verbs

There are apparently only five verbs in this class. They all have the same meaning, namely, 'to cause to do, make to do, bring about'. Nevertheless, they cannot all be used interchangeably. The five verbs are: *mú, dá, sọ, fi,*[1] *ṣe*.

Ó mú mi ṣe bẹ́ẹ̀.	(He made me do so.)
Ó dá ẹ̀rín pa mí.	(He made me laugh.)
Wọ́n sọ ọ́ di ọ̀gá.	(They made him a master.)
Ó fi ìyà jẹ mí.	(He made me suffer.)

---

[1]This verb should not be confused with the preposition *fi* with the same spelling and pronunciation, but with a different function and meaning. The preposition *fi* is discussed in **6.30** and **6.31** below. If the causative verb *fi* and the noun directly following it are dropped, what is left would often be ungrammatical. E.g. *Ó fi ìyà jẹ mí.* (He made me suffer.) and **Ò jẹ mí,* which is meaningless. The preposition *fi* and its object can always be dropped without producing ungrammaticality.

Ó ṣe ikú pa ọ̀rẹ́ rẹ̀.   (He brought about his friend's death.)

For more on Causative Verbs, see **8.24** below.

4.22 Symmetrical Verbs

The subject and object of each of the verbs in this class are freely interchangeable, without appreciable difference (if any at all) in meaning. It is for this reason that the verbs are said to be symmetrical. The class is small in size, being made up of the following verbs:

bí	(literal meaning uncertain)
ṣẹ́	(literal meaning uncertain)
jẹ	(literal meaning uncertain)
bà	(literal meaning uncertain)
kán	(literal meaning uncertain)
pọ́n	(literal meaning uncertain)
ṣe	(literal meaning uncertain)
tì	(literal meaning uncertain)
já	(literal meaning uncertain)
ta	(literal meaning uncertain)
sí	(not to be)
dùn	(be sweet)

Inú bí mi.
Mo bí inú.   (I was angry.)

Ìṣẹ́ ń ṣẹ́ mi.
Mo ń ṣẹ́ ìṣẹ́.   (I am privation.)

Ìyà ń jẹ mí.
Mo ń jẹ ìyà.   (I am suffering.)

Ẹ̀rù bà mí.
Mo ba ẹ̀rù.   (I was afraid.)

Ojú ń kán mi.
Mo ń kán ojú.   (I am in a hurry.)

Ojú ń pọ́n mi.
Mo ń pọ́n ojú.   (I suffer privation.)

Wèrè ń ṣe é.
Ó ń ṣe wèrè.   (He is mad.)

Iyọ̀ dun ọbẹ̀ náà.
Ọbẹ̀ náà dun iyọ̀.   (The stew has the right amount of salt in it.)

Ó ń ti ojú.

Ojú ń tì í.   (He is bashful.)

Mo já àyà.

Àyà já mi.   (I was afraid.)

Ó ta òṣì.

Òṣì ta á.   (He was poor.)

Ara ń ta Òjó.

Òjó ń ta ara.   (Ojo was. full of anxiety.)

Ó ṣe àánú mi.

Àánú mi ṣe é.   (He had pity on me.)

Owó kò sí ní ọwọ́ mi.

Kò sí owó ní ọwọ́ mi.   (I have no money.)

For more on Symmetrical Verbs, see **8.23** below.

4.23   Interrogative Verbs

This is the class of verbs used for asking questions. There are
only two of them, *viz*)

dà   (where is?)

ńkọ́   (where is, how about?)

Owó dà?   (Where is the money (for it)?)

Èyí ńkọ́?   (How about this one?)

4.24   Imperative Verbs

The verbs in this class are used almost exclusively for greetings
and requests. Greetings and requests are a form of command,
using command in a very wide sense. Hence the verbs are
here referred to as imperative verbs. They are:

kú, pẹ̀lẹ́/ǹlẹ́/wẹ̀ẹ́, jọ̀wọ́/jọ̀ọ́ and dákun.

Ẹ kú odò o.   (greeting for people found by the
                           riverside.)

Ẹ pẹ̀lẹ́ sà.   (Hello sir.)

Ẹ jọ̀ọ́ sà.   (Please sir.)

Ẹ dákun o.   (Please!)

For more on Verbs, see **5.33** below.

COMPREHENSION

1. What is the function of verbs in sentences?
2. How many verbs occur in a simple sentence?
3. What kinds of sentences are not simple? How ar they formed?
4. What actually tells speakers what are verbs in the language?
5. Why is it possible for speakers to tell what are verbs in sentences they are hearing for the first time ever?
6. How are new verbs formed in the language?
7. Are there any verbs that are never used with subjects?
8. Do all verbs take the same nouns as subject? If not, why not?
9. Do all verbs take exactly the same number of nouns as subject? If not, why not?
10. Which of the following three verbs can take the greatest number of nouns as subject: *wà, mò, rò*?
11. What verbs are never used with objects in the language?
12. Mention some verbs that are always used with objects.
13. When does the low tone of monosyllabic verbs change to mid-tone?
14. Why are some verbs said to be splitting verbs?
15. In what way are complex verbs complex?
16. What are adjectivisable verbs?
17. What are report verbs used for?
18. What are interrogative verbs, and how many of them are in the language?
19. What are imperative verbs? Why are they given that name?

EXERCISES

A Make a comprehensive list of the nouns that can function as the subject of each of the following verbs when no object is present:

fà	(to creep, be slimy)
gbó	(to be old, to mature)
rò	(to think)
rí	(to find)
jè	(to go about in search of food)

lọ	(to go)
so	(to bear fruit)
yọ́	(to melt)

B There are at least three distinct verbs written and pronounced as *ṣẹ́* in the language. The verbs are differentiated by (1) their meanings and (2) the kinds of nouns that function as their subject and object. For each of the verbs, give its meaning and two lists of nouns that function as its subject and as its object. Make such lists as full as possible.

Do the same thing for the verbs written and pronounced as:

jẹ, wà, rọ̀, wá, kọ, sé, tì, kà and *lé*.

C *Sè* is an adjectivisable verb because we have:

> Ó se iṣu.
> iṣu sísè.

But, by contrast, *rí* is not an adjectivisable verb because we have only the first of the following in the language:

> Ó rí iṣu.
> *iṣu rírí.

Similarly, *gbọ́* is a report verb, because we can say:

> Mo gbọ́ pé Òjó ti dé.

while *sè* is not such a verb, because we do not say:

> *Mo sè pé Òjó ti dé.

Applying tests like the ones given as examples here, draw up for each of the classes of verbs discussed in sections **4.12** to **4.22** two lists, one of the verbs that belong in such a class, and the other of verbs that do not belong there. Make both lists as full as possible.

D Mention three important syntactic inferences that have been drawn in this book from the tone change undergone by low-tone verbs before their objects.

E Identify as many verbs as you can in the following passage[1] and group them according to their sub-classes:

> Ọ̀rọ̀ tí Àjàní sọ wọ Àṣàkẹ́ létí. Ó ní òun rí i pé òdodo ni àlàyé tí Àjàní ṣe. Inú Àjàní dùn. Bí ó tilẹ̀ jẹ́ pé ohun tí ó lè gbe Àjàní l'ó ńsọ fún Àṣàkẹ́, síbẹ̀ ọ̀nà tí ó gbà gbé ọ̀rọ̀ náà kalẹ̀ wọ ni létí púpọ̀. Bí Àṣàkẹ́ bá le mu ìmọ̀ràn yì lò, àti máa lọ s'ọ́dọ̀ Àjàní kò níí ṣòro mọ́. Kẹ̀kẹ̀ bẹ́ẹ̀ imú ẹlẹ́dẹ̀ á wọgbà. Àṣàkẹ́ ní oun á bẹ̀rẹ̀ sí í máa ṣ'àlàyé ọ̀rọ̀ fun bàbá òun, ṣùgbọ́n pé díẹ̀díẹ̀ ni òun yíó máa ṣe é o. Ijó tí a bá gùn kọ́ ni a ńkan ọ̀run. Nwọ́n fi ipade sí ọjọ́ kejì ní yunifásítì ni yàrà Àjàní.

F Find out what is wrong with the following utterances, and then correct them.

1. Iyọ̀ pa ọbẹ̀ rẹ̀.
2. Ògiri náà ti ṣubú.
3. Ìwà Òjó wu Akin púpọ̀, nítorí náà ni Akin fi fẹ́ ẹ.
4. Ó fi abẹ fá ẹsẹ̀ irun rẹ̀.
5. Àlàyé tí o ṣe yẹn kò mọ́ sí mi; nítorí náà o gbọ́dọ̀ tún un ṣe ni.
6. Ó kẹ́ ọdẹ sí 'lẹ̀ fún ọtá rẹ̀.
7. Ó sọ ìmọ̀ràn kan tí kò wá 'yé rárá.
8. Mo dá a ní ìyànjú pé kí o tètè lọ.
9. Ó ń ṣe èrò láti lọ ìdálẹ̀.
10. Ọtí ń mú ẹ ni, àbí kí l'ó ń ṣe ẹ?

---

[1] A. Iṣọla, *Ó le kú*, Ibadan: OUP., 1974, pp. 10–11.

CHAPTER 5

Modifiers

5.1 Any word or phrase which modifies a verb or a sentence is a modifier.

ACTUAL FUNCTION

5.2 When modifiers modify sentences, they create the background against which the meanings of the sentences are to be understood.   For example:

Ṣé ó sọ bẹ́ẹ̀?   (Did he say so?)

In this sentence, *ṣé* is used to signify that the sentence *ó sọ bẹ́ẹ̀* (He said so), must be interpreted as a question and not as just a piece of information.

5.3 With a few exceptions (see **8.30** below), every verb is always accompanied by at least one modifier (see **5.11** below).
   Modifiers are to verbs what qualifiers are to nouns. Modifiers restrict the meanings of verbs by specifying such things as the time, place, manner, condition, etc., in which the actions referred to by verbs were, or are to be, carried out. Thus, the meaning of the sentence:

Òjó lọ.   (Ojo went.)

in which there is only one modifier[1] is a lot broader than that of:

Òjó lọ ní kíákíá.   (Ojo went without delay.)

in which two modifiers are present.

ADVERBS AND ADVERBIALS

5.4 A modifier which in its full form consists of just one word is an adverb, and one which similarly consists of two words

---

[1] See **5.11** below.

or more is an adverbial phrase or an adverbial for short. Thus, *ṣé* above is an adverb, while *ní kíákíá* is an adverbial phrase.

Length or complexity of structure is by no means the only difference between adverbs and adverbials, however. Indeed, they sometimes cannot be distinguished at all on the basis of length, as in:

Òjó lọ rí.	(Ojo went there before.)
Òjó lọ kíákíá.	(Ojo went there quickly.)

in which the word *rí* ((ever) before) is an adverb and *kíákíá* (quickly) is an adverbial.

The real or crucial difference between adverbs and adverbials is that the former cannot be moved from their normal place of occurrence in sentences, whereas the latter can. Thus, the first of the above two examples cannot be turned into:

*rí ni Òjó lọ

But, by contrast, the second example can be turned into:

kíákíá ni Òjó lọ   (Ojo went there without delay.)

5.5 An adverbial phrase in its full form is normally made up of *(i)* a preposition and *(ii)* a noun or nominalisation (with or without a qualifier) functioning as the preposition's object. For example:

ní kíákíá	(without delay)
ní bí mo ti ń wò ẹ́ yìí	(as I am looking at you right now)

in which *ní* is a preposition and *kíákíá* and *bí mo ti ń wò ẹ́ yìí* are noun and noun phrase respectively. An adverbial in its reduced form consists of a noun (with or without qualifiers) only; for example:

kíákíá	(without delay)
bí mo ti ń wò ẹ́ yìí	(as I am looking at you right now)

CLASSIFICATION

5.6 Modifiers are of two principal kinds, namely, verbal modifiers and sentential modifiers.

5.7 Verbal Modifiers

This class in turn consists of two main sub-classes, namely, modifiers that occur before verbs, and modifiers that occur after verbs or their objects. The modifiers that occur before verbs are of two kinds: pre-verbal adverbs and pre-verbal adverbials. The modifiers that occur after verbs are also of two kinds: post-verbal adverbs and post-verbal adverbials.

5.8 Pre-Verbal Adverbs

These adverbs occur between subjects and verbs. For example:

Mo tètè lọ.   (I went without delay.)

where *mo* is subject, *lọ* is verb, and *tètè* is pre-verbal adverb.

The Pre-Verbal Adverbs in the language number between forty and fifty. They are:

yóò	(will, shall)	
óò	(will, shall)	
máa	(will, shall)	Future action/Habi-
á	(will, shall)	tual action
níí[1]	(will, shall (not))	
í	(past/present action	
ti		
tí	(already, completed action)	
ń	(-ing; habitual action, continuous action)	
máa	habitual or continuous action	
a	habitual action in present/past	
ì	(should (have), unaccomplished action)	
báà	(even if)	
ba		
baà	(may)	
lè	(may)	
gbọ́dọ̀	(must)	
tètè	(quickly, without delay)	

---

[1] Yoruba poets sometimes take great liberty with this Adverb by using it like this: *Ojú ò ní ọ ọ́ tì.* (May you never be shamed). The normal, un- distorted form of this sentence is *Ojú ò níí tì ọ́.* (May you never be shamed).

mòómò ⎤	
dìídì ⎦	(intentionally, knowingly, purposely)
ṣìn	(still)
pàpà	(still)
kúkú	(had better, rather, indeed, anyway)
ṣèṣè	(just now, just this minute)
mà	(indeed, in fact)
tiè ⎤	
tilè ⎦	(even)
tún ⎤	
túbò ⎬	(again)
ṣáà ⎦	
sáà)	(anyway, for no purpose, for fun)
dédé	(suddenly, without reason)
wulè	(in vain, to no avail)
jàjà	(at last, finally)
jọ ⎤	
dìjọ ⎬	(together)
jùmọ ⎦	
sì	(consecutive action)
dè	(consecutive action)
nìkan	(alone, single handed)[1]
lè	(be able)
kọ́ ⎤	
kọ́kọ́ ⎦	(first)
jẹ́	(had better)
kàn	(just, simply)
bá	(then, thereupon)
máà	(do not)
sábà	(be in the habit of)

---

[1] Notice that *nìkan* can also occur as a qualifier; see **3.11** above. This is why the sentence *Òjó nìkan jẹun*, is ambiguous in written form, but not when spoken. In one of its meanings/pronunciations, the sentence contains the pre-verbal adverb *nìkan*, while in the other it contains the qualifier *nìkan*. The sentence can correspondingly be 'emphasized' in these two particular forms. *Òjó nìkan ni ó jẹun*, with *nìkan* as a qualifier, and *Òjó ni ó nìkan jẹun*, with *nìkan* as an adverb. The former means 'Ojo was the only one who ate', while the latter means 'Ojo was the one who ate alone'.

kò
ò
ì   (not)
ẹ̀
à
ọ̀n

Òjó á lọ.   (Ojo will go.)
Òjó bá lọ.   (Ojo then went.)
Òjó tiẹ̀ lọ.   (Ojo even went.)
àìlọ (= à-ì-lọ)   (failure to go)   (Cf àlọ='going')

5.9 A sentence can have more than one pre-verbal adverb
in it. For example:

Òjó kò tiẹ̀ lọ.   (Ojo didn't even go.)
Òjó ì bá lọ.   (Ojo would have gone.)
Òjó tiẹ̀ gbọ́dọ̀ tètè máa lọ.   (Ojo even has to get going
                                 soon.)

5.10 Pre-verbal adverbs do not co-occur just any how. They
always occur, arranged one after another, in patterns that
are considered permissible on the grounds of style or of
meaning. For example, the ones that occur in the last example
above probably can be re-arranged as follows:

Òjó gbọ́dọ̀ tiẹ̀ tètè máa lọ.
Òjó gbọ́dọ̀ tètè tiẹ̀ máa lọ.

But they are definitely not allowed to co-occur as in:

*Òjó gbọ́dọ̀ máa tètè tiẹ̀ lọ.

(An asterisk is used to mark examples that are considered to
be incorrect, ungrammatical, or unacceptable). A full discussion and exemplification of this aspect of pre-verbal adverbs
is beyond the scope of the present book. It will be undertaken
elsewhere.

5.11 As can be seen from the translations or glosses given
above, pre-verbal adverbs convey different kinds of meanings.
Attention is called to the following meanings and the pre-
verbal adverbs employed to convey them.

70

Future Action. In positive sentences, future action is signified by the presence of any one of *yóò, óò, á máa* and *ń/* (when the verb is *bò* (to come)).

A máa lọ ní ọla.   (We shall go tomorrow.)

In negative sentences (containing *kò* (not)), future action is signified with *níí*. For example:

A ò níí lọ ní ọla.   (We shall not go tomorrow.)

For more on the markers of future action, see **2.21** above.

Past/Present Action. This is conveyed by *í*. This adverb changes its form with the context, with the result that it can actually also be heard as any of the other vowels in the language. For example:

Ilè ẹ́ gbẹ.   (The ground is dry.)
Oúnjẹ ẹ́ wà.   (There is food.)
Wọn ón lọ.   (They went.)

For many speakers, the adverb in its appropriate contextual form often replaces the last sound of the subject, when that sound has a mid tone. Hence the last two examples above also occur as:

Oúnjẹ́ wà.   (There is food.)
Wọ́n lọ.   (They went.)

With most verbs, the adverb's meaning is past action only, as in:

Dàda á lọ.   (Dada went.)
Dàda á wá.   (Dada came.)

But with many of the members of the class of adjectivisable verbs (see **4.16** above), the adverb indicates either past or present action depending upon the context. For example:

Dàda á ga.   (Dada is/was tall.)
Òwe é ṣòro.   (Proverbs are/were difficult.)

The adverb is left understood rather than being physically represented (technically: it is represented by a zero variant) before the verbs *dà* (where is?) and *ńkọ́* (where is?) and the adverbs *kò* (not), *í* (unaccomplished action), and *a* (habitual action). For example:

Oúnjẹ dà?   (Where is food?/Give me some food.)

71

Oúnjẹ kò sí.	(There is no food around.)
Ilẹ̀ ì bá gbẹ.	(The ground would have been dry.)

It is similarly left understood after the four polymorphic nouns *mo, o, a* and *ẹ*. For example:

Mo lọ.	(I went.)
Ẹ lọ.	(You (pl.) went.)

The adverb regularly merges with the polymorphic noun *ó* (he, she, it), just as it does with the final high tone syllable of subject nouns. For example:

Ó lọ.	(He went)
Òjó lọ.	(Ojo went)

The adverb does not occur at all in direct commands. It occurs optionally in indirect commands. For example:

Dàda, lọ. ·	(Dada, go!)
Ó ní kí Dàda lọ.	(He asked Dada to go.)
Ó ní kí Dàda á lọ.	(He asked Dada to go.)

It similarly does not occur at all (technically: it does not even have a zero variant) in timeless sentences (see **8.30** below). For example:

Èjì dín l'ógún.	(lit. two be-short-of twenty i.e. 'eighteen'.)
Ẹ̀wọ̀n já ní 'bi ̇ ó wù ú.	(The chain breaks just wherever it pleases.)

Any sentence in the language apart from timeless sentences must contain either an appropriate form of the adverb *i* or a marker of future action. In other words, except in timeless sentences, the time of the performance of the action referred to by the verb in any sentence in the language always has to be specified as either past/present or future.

Past/present and future are alternatives, in the sense that if a person selects one of them, he must leave or forgo the other. This being the case, the adverb *i* and the markers for future action should not be able to occur together. This is indeed the case with *yóò, óò, ó,* and *á;* these never occur with the adverb *i,* and vice versa. For example:

Dàda óò lọ.	(Dada will go.)
Dàda á lọ.	(Dada will go.)

72

Contrary to expectation, however, the future marker *máa* and the adverb *í* regularly co-occur, as:

Dàda á máa lọ.   (Dada will go.)
Dadá máa lọ.   (Dada will go.)

For this, the present book has no satisfactory explanation to offer.[1]

Continuous Action.   This is an action that goes on as the on-looker speaks. It is signified with *ń/* and *máa*.

Mò ń sọ̀rọ̀ lọ́wọ́.   (I am busy talking.)
Máa mu ún.   (Be drinking it.)

Habitual Action.   Habitual action, something done by habit, is signified with *yóò, óò, á, a, ń/, máa, ń/,* and *níí.*

Yóò jí, yóò sì gbá gbogbo
ilé.   (She would get up and sweep
                                    the whole house.)
Bí o kí i, kò níí dáhùn.   (If you greeted him, he would
                                    not respond.)
Mo máa ń dé 'bẹ̀ ní 'gbà
kọ̀ọ̀kan.   (I go there once in a while.)

Completed Action.   This is an action that has been completed by the time the speaker starts to talk. It is signified with *ti* and *tí.*

Ó ti lọ bí?   (Has he gone yet?)
Ó tí ì lọ bí?   (Has he gone yet?)

Consecutive Action.   A consecutive action is one that follows another. The pre-verbal adverbs used to indicate this are *sì, dẹ̀, bá,* and *báà.*

---

[1] It may be pointed out for whatever it is worth, however, that in English, present tense forms can co-occur with future time reference, as is the case in Yoruba. When that happens, the meaning conveyed thereby is solely that of future time reference, again, exactly as in Yoruba. Thus, the verb 'goes' in 'He goes' is marked as present. But in the sentence 'He goes tomorrow' the action of going can only be interpreted as one which will take place in the future. Cf. 'He is going now'. and 'He is going tomorrow'. It would thus seem from these English examples that the anomaly involved in the present/past action marker's co-occurring with the future marker is not peculiar to the Yoruba language.

The first three indicate that some action or actions occurred earlier, while the fourth indicates that some action or actions will follow. For example:

Òjó bá kúkú jókòó.   (There and then, Ojo simply sat down.)

Òjó sì dìde.   (In addition, Ojo got up.)

Òjó ì báà lọ,......   (Even if Ojo goes,......)

Commands. Some kinds of commands, injunctions, or exhortations are signified with *máa* and *máà (má)*.

Máa lọ.   (Go on!)

Máà (Má) lọ.   (Don't go!)

Correction. False or untrue statements are corrected with *mà*. The end of a sentence containing this pre-verbal adverb always sounds differently from the end of the same sentence without the adverb. For example:

Ó lọ.   (He went.)

Ó mà lọọ.   (As a matter of fact, he went.)

Ó dé.   (He returned.)

Ó mà déè.   (In fact, he returned.)

PRE-VERBAL ADVERBIALS

5.12 The adverbials in this class are only three in number. They are those introduced by the following prepositions:

ti   (from)

bá   (for, in company with, on behalf of)

fi   (with, by means of)

5.13 Adverbials containing the preposition *ti* are used to indicate the point in space or time from which things come and events begin. For example:

Ó ti Èkó dé ní àná.   (He got back from Lagos yesterday.)

Ó ti àárọ̀ bẹ̀rẹ̀ ìwà burúkú.   (He began behaving badly right from his youth.)

5.14 Adverbials beginning with the preposition *bá* are used to signify accompaniment or the beneficiaries usually of other people's actions. For example:

Ó bá mi ra bàtà bọ̀. (He bought a pair of shoes for me from there.)

Ẹ bá mi pè é. (Please, call him/her for me.)

5.15 Adverbials beginning with *fi* signify manner, or the means by which an action is accomplished. For example:

Ó fi ayọ̀ gbà á. (He received it gladly.)

Ó fi ọ̀bẹ ha á. (He scraped it with a knife.)

5.16 The adverbials in this class co-occur with each other freely. For example:

Ó ti ibí bá mi fi ọkọ̀ kó o. (From here he helped me move it by lorry.)

Ó bá mi ti ibí fi ọkọ̀ kó o. (He helped me move it from here by lorry.)

Ó fi ọkọ̀ ti ibí bá mi kó o lọ. (He helped me move it from here by lorry.)

Furthermore, they co-occur with the pre-verbal adverbs. When that happens, adverbials occur next to the verbs. For example:

Wọn ò tètè ti Èkó dé. (They didn't get back from Lagos early.)

Mo tilẹ̀ fi ọ̀bẹ ha á. (I even scraped it with a knife.)

POST-VERBAL ADVERBS

5.17 As said earlier when defining this class, post-verbal adverbs occur after the verbs they modify, or after the objects of such verbs. The class is comparatively small, being made up of the following adverbs only:

mọ́	(any more, ever (again)).
rí	(ever (before))
rárá	(at all)
sáá	(in vain)

gan-an	(really, extremely)[1]
wàyí	(now, right now)

A ò rí wọn mọ́.	(We cannot find them any more.)
Ọwọ́ tẹ́ ọ́ wàyí.	(Now you have been caught.)
Ó wù mí gan-an.	(I like it a great deal.)

5.18 Some of these adverbs can co-occur, while others cannot. Furthermore, some of them, on account of their meanings, cannot occur in the same sentence with some of the pre-verbal adverbs discussed above.

POST-VERBAL ADVERBIALS

5.19 The post-verbal adverbials are four in number. They are the adverbials introduced by the following prepositions:

ní	(in, at, to, on)	fún	(for, on behalf of)
sí	(in, at, to)	pẹ̀lú	(with)

5.20 Adverbials introduced by the preposition *ní* are the most numerous in the language. They are used to signify the following kinds of meanings: time, location, manner, appearance, condition, circumstance, direction, aspect or respect.

5.21 It is either possible or actually obligatory to drop the preposition *ní* in some contexts. For this reason, the adverbials that it introduces often occur without the preposition itself being physically present. In the following examples, the preposition will be put in brackets in those contexts where it can be dropped, and marked with an asterisk where it must be dropped.

---

[1] The word *gan-an* also occurs as a qualifier in the language; see **3.11** above. This is why the sentence *Mo fẹ́ràn rẹ̀ gan-an* is ambiguous. In one of its meanings it contains the adverb *gan-an*, while in the other it contains the qualifier *gan-an*. When *gan-an* is an adverb, the sentence means 'I like him/her a lot', but when *gan-an* is a qualifier, it means 'I like him/her in particular'. These two meanings become clearer and more obvious when 'emphasis' occurs, viz. *Òun ni mo fẹ́ràn gan-an* (He/She is the one I like a lot), and *Òun gan-an ni mo fẹ́ràn* (He/She in particular is the one I like).

i. Preposition cannot be dropped

Ó wá ní àárọ̀.	(He came in the morning.)
Mo rí i ní ibẹ̀.	(I saw him there.)
Ayé ń lọ ní mẹ̀lọmẹ̀lọ.	(Life went on smoothly.)
Nǹkan ń lọ ní ṣíṣè-n-tẹ̀lé.	(Things progressed in an orderly manner.)

ii. Preposition can be dropped

Ó ṣòro (ní) 'íṣe.	(It is difficult to do.)
A lọ (ní) kíákíá.	(We went without delay.)
Ó sọ ilẹ̀ (ní) kùù.	(It struck the ground with a heavy sound.)
Kò rìn (ní) ìhòhò.	(He didn't walk in the nude.)
Ó rí (ní) roboto.	(It is round in appearance.)
A ó rí i (ní ìgbà) tí ó bá padà.	(We shall see him when he gets back.)
Jáde (ní) bí mo ti ń wò ẹ́ yìí!	(Get out right now!)
Mo fẹ́ ẹ (ní) bẹ́ẹ̀.	(I want it like that.)

iii. Preposition must be dropped

Ó yẹ *ní kí á lọ kí i.	(We ought to go and greet him.)
Mo mọ̀ *ní pé ó wá.	(I know that he was present.)
*Ní bí òjò bá rọ̀, ìyàn kò níí mú.	(If it rains, there will be no famine.)
Mo sọ *ní bẹ́ẹ̀.	(I said so.)
Wọ́n fẹ́ràn rẹ̀ *ní jákèjádò ilẹ̀ yìí.	(People like him all over this country.)
Ti *ní òsán ti *ní òru.	(Both day and night.)

5.22 Adverbials with the preposition *sí* are used to signify location, time, and direction of movement.[1] For example:

Ó lọ sí oko.	(He went to his farm.)
Ó bí ọmọ sí ilé.	(She has children at home.)
A fi ìpàdé wa sí ọ̀la.	(We have fixed our meeting for tomorrow.)

---

[1] The preposition *sí* can sometimes be left out of sentences; as in:
Ó lọ Ìbàdàn = *Ó lọ sí Ìbàdàn* (He/She went to Ibadan).

77

5.23 Although both *sí* and *ní* are used to signify location, there is nevertheless a very subtle difference between the locational meanings conveyed by the two prepositions. For example:

Ó kú sí oko.	(He died and was (probably) burried in his farm.)
Ó kú ní oko.	(He died on his farm but was (probably) burried elsewhere.)
Ó dúró sí ibẹ̀.	(He waited there.)
Ó dúró ní ibẹ̀.	(He stopped briefly there.)

5.24 Adverbials with the preposition *fún* are used to signify the beneficiaries of verbal actions. For this reason, sentences with such adverbials often have the same meaning as those having adverbials with *bá*.

Pè é fún mi. ⎫
Bá mi pè é. ⎬   (Call him for me.)

5.25 Adverbials with the preposition *pẹ̀lú* are used to express manner or circumstance. Clear and unexceptionable instances of such adverbials are very hard to find.

Ó ṣe é pẹ̀lú túláàsì.   (He was forced to do it.)

5.26 The post-verbal adverbials can co-occur. For example:

Ó jù ú sí ibẹ̀ fún mi ní àná. (He threw it there for me yesterday.)

Furthermore, they can occur with the post-verbal adverbs. When that happens, they appear in the order:

Verb (Object) + Post-Verbal Adverbials + Post-Verbal Adverbs.

For example:

Kò jù ú sí ibẹ̀ fún mi rí.   (He has never thrown it there for me before.)

SENTENTIALS

5.27 The sententials consist of adverbs and adverbials which modify sentences. Some sententials occur only at the beginning of sentences, others only at the end of sentences, and still others at either the beginning or the end of sentences.

5.28 Sentence-Initial Sententials

These are the sententials that occur at the beginning of sentences only. Examples are:

ǹjẹ́	(?)
ṣé	(?) } (for asking questions)
àní	(I mean, in other words, as already indicated)
àṣé	(no wonder) (for asking rhetorical questions)
kàkà kí ó wá	(instead of him coming)
Ǹjẹ́ o rí i?	(Did you find it?)
Àní kò wá.	(He didn't come. That's what I am telling you.)
Àṣé bẹ́ẹ̀ ni?	(So, that's the way it is?)

5.29 Sentence-final Sententials

These sententials occur at the end of sentences only. They are:

o	(occurs most especially in greetings)
pàápàá	(especially, moreover, considering)
bí	(?) (for asking questions)
kẹ̀	(of all things/people) (shows contempt)
sẹ́	(as already indicated)
mànà	(for sure, definitely)
pẹ̀lú	(in addition)
bóyá ó wá tàbí kò wá	(whether he came or he didn't come)
bí Òjó bá wá	(whether Ojo came)
Tìrẹ ti jẹ́ kẹ̀?	(Why should someone like you be bothering me?)
Kò dé ibẹ̀ rí sẹ́.	(As I've already told you, he has never been there before.)

79

Èyí wù ẹ́ bí?   (Do you like this one?)
Mo fẹ́'ẹ́mọ̀ bóyá   (I want to know whether he
  ó wá tàbí kò wá.   came or he didn't come.)
Ó dàbọ̀ o!   (So long!)

5.30 Sentence-Initial/Final Sententials

The sententials which can occur either at the beginning or at the end of sentences consist mostly of adverbials from which the preposition *ní* is almost always dropped in the present form of the language. Examples of the sententials in this class are:

síbẹ̀síbẹ̀	(still, nevertheless)
ní àìsí àníàní	(undoubtedly, definitely)
ní tòótọ́	(in truth)
bí ó ti wù kí ó rí	(whatever the case may be)
kí a sọ tòótọ́	(to be frank, be truthful)
bí Ọjó bá wá	(if Ojo comes)
kí á ní Òjó wá	(if Ojo had come)
ìbá ṣe pé Òjó wá	(if Ojo had come)
à bá ní Òjó wá	(if Ojo had come)
ì báà wá	(even if he comes)
dípò pé kí ó wá	(instead of him coming)

Síbẹ̀síbẹ̀, mà á wá. Mà á wá síbẹ̀síbẹ̀.	(Still, I'll come.)
Kí á sọ tòótọ́, ọkùnrin ni. Ọkùnrin ni, kí á sọ tòótọ́.	(To be truthful, he is a courageous man.)
Ẹ ó rí mi, bí Òjó bá wá. Bí Òjó bá wá, ẹ ó rí mi.	(You'll see me if Ojo comes.)
Ẹ ò níí rí mi, ì báà wá. Ì báà wá, ẹ ò níí rí mi.	(You won't see me, even if he comes.)

5.31 Most of the sententials described as part of adverbial phrases in the foregoing sections are referred to as adverbial clauses of manner, condition, etc. in traditional grammar. The difference between the present book and traditional grammars of the language is both one of emphasis and of fact. To see this, consider the sentence:

80

Ẹ ó rí mi, bí Òjó bá wá.   (You will see me if Ojo comes.)

Traditional grammars place emphasis on the form of the sentential *bí Òjó bá wá*, and therefore call it an adverbial clause of condition. The present book on the other hand places emphasis on function and therefore analyses the sentential as a noun or nominalisation functioning as the object of a deleted preposition *ní*.

Traditional grammars would call *bí* in that sentential a subordinating conjunction employed to subordinate the sentence *Òjó bá wá* (Ojo then came) to the main sentence *Ẹ ó rí mi* (You will see me). In the present book, *bí* is an introducer used to turn the sentence *Òjó bá wá* into a noun/nominalisation.

That *bí Òjó bá wá* is a noun/nominalisation, as claimed in this book, is shown by the fact that it can be used as a noun in its present form and meaning. Thus as a rejoinder to the above sentence, one can say,

Bí Òjó bá wá kò wọ ọ̀rọ̀   (The condition that Ojo must
yìí o. Kí o wá dandan   also be present is out of the
ni mo fẹ́.   question. I want you to come
                              regardless of what Ojo does.)

One can also say,

Ọ̀rọ̀ bí Òjó bá wá kọ́ o.   (It's not a matter of whether
                              Ojo is present or not.)

where *bí Òjó bá wá* is a genitival qualifier, and the latter, as already pointed out (see **3.15** above), is derived from nouns only.

Finally, the sentence *Ẹ ó rí mi bí Òjó bá wá* can also be said in this way, with essentially the same meaning:

Ẹ ò níí rí mi àfi bí Òjó   (You will not see me, unless
bá wá.   Ojo comes.)

Now, as indicated in **7.9** below, the disjunction *àfi* joins or precedes nouns/nominalisations and adverbials only. It precedes *bí Òjó bá wá* in the above sentence; hence *bí Òjó bá wá* is either a noun/nominalisation or an adverbial.[1]

If *bí Òjó bá wá* is a noun, then the question arises as to the precise function it performs in the sentence:

Ẹ ó rí mi, bí Òjó bá wá.

Now, this sentence has a subject already, in the form of *ẹ*. Therefore *bí Òjó bá wá* cannot be a subject noun there. The sentence also has an object already, in the form of *mi*. Therefore, again, *bí Òjó bá wá* cannot be an object noun. If the nominalisation *bí Òjó bá wá* is neither a subject nor an object in its sentence, then it has to be the object of a preposition, since this is the only other function available to it there. (Cf. the definition of nouns in **2.1** above). This is why this book analyses some of the sententials cited in the foregoing sections as nouns/ nominalisations functioning as the object of a deleted or deletable preposition.

That preposition is specifically identified as *ní* partly because of the meanings that those sententials convey, and partly because of the existence of the following examples:

ní kí aṣáájú sòrò, kí á bá òrò náà bẹ́ẹ̀. . . . .   (for a leader to say something and for one to find what he has said to be the truth. . . .)

Kí a tó lè sòrò ènìyàn kan ní bí a ti sòrò ti olóyè yìí. . . .   (for one to speak as we have spoken about this chief. . . .)

(D.O. Fagunwa, *Àdììtú Olódùmarè*, Nelson, 1962, p. viii)

---

[1] Notice that, in addition to:

Ì báà wá, ẹ ò níí rí mi.   (You won't see me, even if he comes.)

there exist in the language sentences like:

Ì báà wá, kí ó fa àpò kan l'ọwọ́, ẹ ò níí rí mi.   (You won't see me, even if he comes bringing ₦200 with him.)

In this latter sentence, the nominalisation/noun *kí ó fa àpò kan l'ọwọ́*, is a substitute for *ì báà fa àpò kan l'ọwọ́* (even if he brings ₦200 with him). This kind of substitution would not be possible if *ì báà fa àpò kan l'ọwọ́* and *ì báà wá* were not themselves nouns/nominalisations. On the status and function of *kí*, see **6.5** and **6.11** below.

Mú àwọn ẹ̀gbọ́n mi mẹ́fẹ̀ẹ̀- (Restorè all my six brothers to
fà. . . . . padà sí bí wọ́n their original form imme-
ti wà rí ní wéréwéré. diately.)

(D.O. Fagunwa, *Itan Oloyin*, O.U.P., 1963, p. 16)

INTERROGATIVE MODIFIERS

5.32 As is the case with the nouns, the qualifiers, and the verbs, there are modifiers which are used more or less exclusively for asking questions. Such modifiers are found only in the sub-class of sententials. They are: ṣé, ǹjẹ, àṣẹ, and bí. *Ǹjẹ* and *bí* can be used interchangeably; otherwise, these modifiers have different meanings, in the sense that they are used for asking different kinds of questions. Note especially that *àṣé* is used only for asking rhetorical questions; that is, more precisely, questions whose answers are beforehand known even to the interrogator.

OBLIGATORY MODIFIERS

5.33 As there are nouns that cannot normally be used without any accompanying qualifiers, so there are verbs that never occur in grammatical sentences in which no modifiers are present. Such verbs are:

fi[1]   (put)   bẹ   (to be red)
mọ   (to be limited)   rí   (to appear, to seem, to be)
rẹ̀   (to be red)

The modifiers used with these verbs are, respectively:

sí	+	Place Noun
ní	+	Noun/Nominalisation
(ní)	+	dòdò
(ní)	+	yòò
(ní)	+	Manner Noun

Ó fi ìwé rẹ̀ sí ibẹ̀.   (He put his books there.)
Kò mọ ní ìwọn.   (It is excessive.)
Ó rẹ̀ dòdò.   (It is (deep) red in colour.)
Aṣọ náàa bẹ yòò.   (The cloth was bright red in colour.)
Ó rí bí òṣùpá.   (It looks like the moon.)

---

[1]Notice that this is the third *fi* in the language. For the others, see **4.21** above, and **6.30**, **6.31** below.

COMPREHENSION

1. Are modifiers phrases or words or both?
2. Which two of the following do modifiers go with: verbs, nouns, adjectives, sentences and qualifiers?
3. Complete the following statement:
   'Modifiers are to verbs as qualifiers are to ………….'
4. What is an adverb? What is an adverbial? How do these differ from one another?
5. Is there any difference in this book between an adverbial and an adverbial phrase?
6. What do modifiers actually do to the meanings of verbs and sentences?
7. Name the four verbal modifiers set up in this book.
8. What are pre-verbal adverbs? Where do they occur in sentences?
9. How many kinds of pre-verbal adverbials are there in Yoruba?
10. What are post-verbal adverbs? Why are they said to be post-verbal?
11. What meanings do adverbials introduced by the preposition *ni* convey?
12. Is the preposition *ni* obligatory in adverbials? Explain your answer.
13. What are sententials?
14. How many major sub-classes of sententials are there? Name them.
15. Make a list of modifiers used for asking questions.
16. Make a list of verbs that are never used without modifiers.

EXERCISES

A Work out the order in which pre-verbal adverbs co-occur with themselves.
B Construct and employ in sentences grammatical strings of three pre-verbal adverbs and upwards.
C Find out which post-verbal adverbs cannot co-occur.
D Find out which post-verbal adverbs cannot occur in the same sentence with some pre-verbal adverbs.
E What is the basis for the claim that the preposition *ni* can be dropped from the second set of examples given in Section **5.21**?

F What is the basis for the claim that the third set of examples given in Section **5.21** contain a preposition *ní*, and that the preposition is always dropped?

G Construct ten pairs of sentences like the two given in Section **5.23**. Study the difference between the meanings of the members of each pair, and try to establish whether or not the difference in meaning remains constant from one pair to the other.

H Correct the following utterances:

1. 'Fọ eyín rẹ pẹ̀lú àbùfọyín Maclean.'
2. Ó lọ sí ìlú òyìnbó pẹ̀lú ọkọ̀ ojú omi.
3. Pẹ̀lú ayọ̀ àti àláfià ni mo fi kọ ìwé yí sí yín.
4. Ẹ jẹ́ k'á bẹ̀rẹ̀ ìsìn wa pẹ̀lú kíkọ orin ogún.
5. Mo ń bọ̀ sí ọ̀dọ̀ rẹ l'álẹ́.
6. Ó fẹ́ 'ẹlọ sí bàbá rẹ̀.
7. Ǹjẹ́ Òjó wá ní alẹ́ àná bí?
8. Àṣẹ ọmọ náà dà?
9. Aṣọ náà pọ́n láúláú.
10. Wọ́n ti ṣe ètò sí'lẹ̀ l'oríìṣiríìṣi.

85

CHAPTER 6
Introducers

6.1 Most of the words in the language are primarily members of one or the other of the four major parts of speech discussed in the preceding four chapters. As such, their normal or primary functions are those regularly associated with the parts of speech to which they belong. Thus, the normal or primary function of a word classified as a noun in Chapter 2 is to function as subject or object. Similarly, the normal function of a word classified as a verb is to function as predicator in sentences.

6.2 However, many words or elements in the language are regularly made to perform what are not their normal or primary functions, as defined above. For example:

Ó wàhálà mi púpọ̀.   (He bothered me a great deal.)

Many educated speakers would say that *wàhálà* in this example is a noun which is 'used as a verb'; that is, in other words, *wàhálà* performs a non-primary function in this sentence.

6.3 When items are made to perform non-primary functions, their forms are either altered in some way to reflect this fact, or left completely unchanged. Introducers are the items employed for marking or altering the forms of elements performing non-primary functions in sentences. Introducers normally appear to the left of the elements they mark.

6.4 Introducers for Nouns
Elements that are made to function non-primarily as nouns are not always so marked. For example:

'Lọ' tí o kọ kò dára tó.   (The 'lọ' that you wrote is not good enough.)

86

Ọ̀rọ̀ di bí o ò lọ o yà 'ún mi.　(The situation became one in
　　　　　　　　　　　　　　　which each person started
　　　　　　　　　　　　　　　struggling to save his own
　　　　　　　　　　　　　　　life only.)
Ó dé ti àìdé, ...　　　　　(He had scarcely arrived, ...)
Ó mú méjì.　　　　　　　　(He took two.)

In these examples, the verb *lọ*, the sentences *Bí o ò lọ o yà
'ún mi* and *Ó dé*, and the qualifier *méjì* are used as nouns without being so marked in any way.

6.5 When items that are not normally nouns are marked as
functioning as nouns, the introducers employed are:

　i.　o-, e-, ẹ-, ọ-, a
　ii.　a-, ọ̀-, ò-, ì, i, total reduplication
　iii.　à-, Cí-
　iv.　Cí-, à-
　v.　ì-, o-, a-, ọ, à-, è-
　vi.　kí, pé, pékí, bí/tí[1]

6.6 *Examples:*

　(i)　olówó　　(o-ní-owó)　　(wealthy person)
　　　　eléwé　　(o-ní-ewé)　　(leaf-seller)
　　　　ẹléja　　(o-ní-ẹja)　　(fish-seller)
　　　　ọlókọ̀　　(o-ní-ọkọ̀)　　(lorry-owner)
　　　　alájá　　(o-ní-ajá)　　(dog-owner)
　　　　onígi　　(o-ní-igi)　　(wood-seller)

The primary form of the introducer used here is *o*. But this
form changes in a very regular way with the context. The
items which the introducer marks as functioning as nouns
are verb phrases, i.e. combinations of verbs and other things,
in this case, their objects.

---

[1] *Bí*, the introducer, is not to be confused with *bí*, the noun mentioned in
2.6 above. The two *bí*'s are distinct both in function and in meaning.
They behave differently also. Thus, Cf. *Bí Dàda bá lọ* (If Dada goes) (with
the introducer) and *Ó ń ṣe bí i Dàda* (He is behaving like Dada), with the
noun. There are still other *bí*'s in the language; Cf. **4.14**, **4.22** and **5.31**
above.

6.7 *Examples:*

(ii)

a-dájó	(a-dá ẹjọ́)	(a judge)
a-kọ̀wé	(a-kọ ìwé)	(secretary)
ọ̀-dàlẹ̀	(ọ̀-da ilẹ̀)	(a traitor)
ọ̀-lẹ	(ọ̀-lẹ)	(lazy person)
ò-jólé	(ò-jó ilé)	(an arsonist)
ò-jíṣẹ́	(ò-jẹ́ iṣẹ́)	(a messenger)
ì-ránṣẹ́	(ì-rán ní iṣẹ́)	(messenger)
ì-múná	(ì-mú iná)	(pair of pliers or pincers)
ì-kéèjì	(ì-kó èjì)	(the second)
i-pè	(i-pè)	(a bugle)
paná-paná	(pa iná pa iná)	(fire-fighter)
pẹja-pẹja	(pa ẹja pa ẹja)	(fisherman)

The elements marked as functioning as nouns in these examples
are verb phrases. The introducers used do not all have the
same form, but their meanings are similar.

6.8 *Examples:*

(iii)

à-pajẹ (à-pa jẹ)	(thing to be slaughtered for food)
à-bákú (à-bá kú)	(something to be endured until death)
à-bọ́pa (à-bọ́ pa)	(something to be fattened for slaughter)
bí-bọ́pa (bí-bọ́ pa)	
pí-pajẹ (pí-pa jẹ)	(thing to be slaughtered for food)

One of the introducers used here always takes the form of the
initial sound of the element to be transformed, followed by
the sound *í*. The letter *C* in the list of introducers given under
(iii) stands for the initial consonantal sound (whatever it
may be) of the element to be transformed.

6.9 *Examples:*

(iv)

lí-lọ	(lí- lọ)	(the act/fact of going)
kí-kọ́ ilé	(kí - kọ́ ilé)	(building houses)
à-ti-lọ	(à - ti lọ)	(going)
à-tètè-dé	(à - tètè dé)	(early arrival)
à-ti-kọ́ ilé	(à - ti kọ́ ilé)	(building houses)
à-lọ	(à - lọ)	(going, act of going)
à-ì-lọ	(à - ì lọ)	(not going)

One of the two introducers employed here takes the form represented by Cí-, namely, the initial consonantal sound (whatever it may be) of the word to be transformed, followed by *i*. The two introducers mark verb phrases as being used as nouns.

6.10 *Examples:*

(v)	ì-bínú	(ì-bí inú)	(anger)
	ì-rójú	(ì-ró ojú)	(endurance)
	ì-múra	(ì-mú ara)	(preparation)
	o-gbó	(o-gbó)	(old age)
	ọ-gbọ́n	(ọ-gbọ́n)	(wisdom)
	ọ-là	(ọ-là)	(wealth)
	a- gọ̀	(a - gọ̀)	(folly)
	a- fẹ́	(a -fẹ́)	(good life, elegance)
	à - ṣẹ	(à - ṣẹ)	(order)
	à - sè	(à- sè)	(feast)
	à - lá	(à - lá)	(dream)
	è - gbè	(è- gbè)	(chorus)
	è - gbé	(è - gbé)	(destruction, perdition)

Here, as in the immediately preceding example, the elements marked as nouns are verb phrases. The introducers employed have a unified meaning, even though their forms differ rather widely.

It is convenient to point out at this point that it is verb phrases (i.e. combinations of verbs and their objects and/or modifiers) and not just plain verbs that are actually turned into nouns or nominalisations with introducers in Yoruba. To see this, consider the sentence:

Ọ̀rọ̀ lílọ rẹ̀ ni à ń sọ.   (We are discussing his departure.)

The noun/nominalisation *lílọ* is ambiguous in meaning, as it can refer either to a departure that has already taken place or to one that is yet to occur. When the noun refers to a departure that has already occurred, it is derived with the introducer *Cí-* from *i lọ*, a verb phrase in which the indicator of past/present action is marked by the adverb *i*. When, on the other hand, the noun refers to a departure that is yet to take place, it is derived, again with the introducer *Cí-* from something like *á lọ* or *yóò lọ,* a verb phrase with an adverb for indicating future action. These adverbs do not show up physically in the final form of the nouns, but their meanings are there nonetheless. The adverbs do not occur physically in the final form of the nouns apparently because the introducer *Cí-,* among others, cannot co-occur physically with adverbs indicating future action and past/present action.

The same thing is true of the introducer *kí.* Thus, in *Mo fẹ́ kí Òjó lọ* (I want Ojo to go.), Ojo's going is to take place in the future, yet the future marker is physically absent, because of the introducer *kí.*

6.11 *Examples:*

(vi)	kí a sọ tòótọ́	(To be frank, being frank, frankness)
	pé o dé ní àná	(That you got back yesterday)
	pé kí a ṣọ́ra gidigidi	(That we should be very careful)
	bí a bá ṣọ́ra	(If we are careful)
	tí a bá ṣọ́ra	(If we are careful)

All the introducers employed here are for marking full sentences as used as nouns. These introducers are traditionally known as subordinating conjunctions. This term is rejected here as it diverts attention from the similarity between the function of the introducers themselves and that of the other introducers already exemplified or yet to be exemplified.

That the above utterances are nouns/nominalisations rather than clauses, as popularly believed, is shown by at least two facts. First of all, they can function as subject or object in their present form (Cf. **5.31** above). Secondly, given appropriate context, they can be preceded by some conjunctions and disjunctions (see Chapter 7) which precede nouns/nominalisations and adverbials only. For example:

Kí á sọ òótọ́ dára ju pé kí a máa purọ́.	(It is better to be truthful than to be mendacious.)
Pé o dé ní àná yà mí l'ẹ́nu.	(I am surprised that you arrived back yesterday.)
Kinní yìí á yíwọ́ o, àfi bí a bá ṣọ́ra.	(This thing will surely get out of hand unless we are very careful.)

Àti pé kòkó tà àti pé kò tà, ṣe bí ọwọ́ ìjọba ni gbogbo rẹ̀ wà.	(But, as you surely know, whether cocoa beans fetch a good price or not is entirely up to the government.)	

The first two sentences exemplify their use as subject and/or object, while the last two show them preceded by the disjunction *àfi* (unless, except), and the conjunction *àti* (and).

6.12 Nouns of one category can also be made to function as nouns of another category through the help of introducers. There are two categories of nouns produced in this way.

Example:

(a)	ọsọ̀ọ̀sẹ̀	(ọsẹ̀ ọsẹ̀)	(every week)
	ojoojúmọ́	(ojú mọ́ ojú mọ́)	(every day)
	ẹsẹẹsẹ	(ẹsẹ ẹsẹ)	(line by line)
	díẹ̀díẹ̀	(díẹ̀ díẹ̀)	(little by little)
	méjìméjì	(méjì méjì)	(two by two)

The introducer used here takes the form of the total repetition (total reduplication) of the words concerned. Most of the nouns formed as above are manner nouns, i.e. nouns that function primarily as object of the preposition *ní*. A few such nouns can function as the object of other prepositions or even verbs, however. For example:

ọgbọọgbọ́n	(ọgbọ́n ọgbọ́n)	(untranslatable)
ẹ̀gbẹ̀ẹ̀gbẹ́	(ẹ̀gbẹ́ ẹ̀gbẹ́)	(untranslatable)
ẹ̀bẹ̀ẹ̀bá	(ẹ̀bá ẹ̀bá)	(untranslatable)
òwọ̀ọ̀wọ́	(òwọ́ òwọ́)	(different groups)
àgbààgbà	(àgbà àgbà)	(the elders)

Ó fi iṣu sí iná, ó ń fi ọgbọọgbọ́n wá ọbẹ.	(He left yams baking in the fire, and in the meantime began to think of ways of finding a knife.)
Ẹ̀gbẹ̀ẹ̀gbẹ́ ọnà ni ó gbà dé 'bẹ̀.	(He kept to the edge of the road all the way.)

Those of the nouns beginning with vowels invariably have the same vowels and tones in their first three syllables. This is accomplished *(i)* by dropping all but the first two syllables of the first of the two tokens or occurrences of the words combined to form such nouns, and *(ii)* by changing the tone and vowel in the second syllable of that first token, where necessary. Thus, *ojúmọ́ ojúmọ́* first becomes *ojú ojúmọ́*, and then, by vowel and tone change, *ojoojúmọ́*.

6.13 *Example:*

(b)   ọmọkọ́mọ   (ọmọ-kí-ọmọ)   (a good-for-nothing
                                                    child)
         èyànkéèyàn   (ènìyàn-kí-ènìyàn)   (a good-for-nothing
                                                    fellow)
         ìgbàkúùgbà   (ìgbà-kí-ùgbà)   (any time)
         ẹnikẹ́ni   (ẹni-kí-ẹni)   (anyone, anybody)
         ohunkóhun   (ohun-kí-ohun)   (anything)

There is total reduplication here, as in the preceding set of examples. But in addition, an introducer with the form of *kí* is also used. These two introducers jointly mark nouns as decidedly indefinite.

6.14   Introducers for Qualifiers

As in the case of the nouns, many of the elements made to function non-primarily as qualifiers are never so marked. This is always the case with appositive qualifiers (derived from nouns) and genitival qualifiers (also derived from nouns[1]). For example:

     ikú èkejì òrìṣà   (death, God's lieutenant)
     ìwé Òjó   (Ojo's book)

Many adjectives and numerals derived from nouns and some adjectives derived from verb phrases are not formally marked either. For example:

     Omi mímu   (drinking water)
     ẹran títà   (meat that is for sale)
     oṣù méjì   (two months)

Polymorphic nouns assume special forms when functioning as genitival qualifiers. They are therefore an exception to this general observation.

| ẹsẹ̀ ẹ̀kẹ́ẹ̀jọ | (line eight, the eighth line) |
| ènìyàn pupa fòò | (a person that is very light in complexion) |

6.15 When items are specifically marked as qualifiers, the introducers used are: *Cí, tí* and *ni*.

6.16 The introducer *Cí....*, which takes the form of the initial consonantal sound of the element to the trans-formed, followed by *í*, is used for marking verb phrases, i.e. verbs, with or without accompanying objects and/or modifiers, as qualifiers. For example:

gíga	(gí-ga)	(tall)
gíga fiofio	(gí-ga fiofio)	(very tall)
rírú	(rǐ-rú)	(dirty, muddy (water))
kíkẹ̀	(kí-kẹ̀)	(decayed, putrid)
jíjóná	(jí-jó ní inú iná)	(burnt)

As in the case of nouns/nominalisations, adjectives are not derived from plain verbs, but rather from verb phrases. This is so because of the meanings of the adjectives themselves. Thus, the adjective *mímu* in:

> Omi mímu   (drinking water)

refers to an act of drinking that is yet to take place rather than to one that has already occurred. For this reason, the adjective must be described as having come from a verb phrase like ó/óò/máa/lè mu (will/can drink), as in:

> Omi tí a ó/óò/máa/lè mu.   (Water that one can/will drink.)

If the adjective *mímu* had come from the plain verb *mu* (to drink), as is the popular belief, it would have been able to refer to an act of drinking that is yet to occur as well as to one that has already occurred.

Similarly, the adjective *kíkẹ̀* in:

> ẹja kíkẹ̀   (putrid fish)

must, solely because of its meaning, have been derived from the verb phrase *ti kẹ̀/ti ń kẹ̀* (already putrid/already becoming

93

putrid), and not from ó/óò/máa kẹ̀ (will become putrid). In other words, the above phrase has the same meaning as:

ẹja tí ó ti (ń) kẹ̀   (fish that is (becoming) putrid)

rather than as:

ẹja tí ó máa kẹ̀   (fish that will be putrid)

6.17 It is convenient to point out here that, contrary to popular belief, modifiers never modify adjectives in Yoruba. In other words, in the following phrase:

igi gíga fíofío   (a very tall tree)

fíofío does not modify *gíga*. The latter and *fíofío* together constitute the adjective there. The adjective is derived, as indicated above, from the verb phrase *ga fíofío* (be very tall). The adjective *jíjóná* is derived in the same way from the verb phrase *jó ní inú iná* (burn inside fire).

The way adjectives are derived from verb phrases is exactly the same as the way nouns are derived from verb phrases. Thus, in *àsọ tẹ́lẹ̀* (forecast), *àsọ* is not a noun modified by *tẹ́lẹ̀* (before). Rather, it is the entire utterance *àsọtẹ́lẹ̀* that is a noun. It was formed from the verb phrase *sọ tẹ́lẹ̀* (to say beforehand).

THE INTRODUCER *tí*

6.18 The introducer *tí* marks sentences that are used as (relative clause) qualifiers. As is expected of most introducers, *tí* always appears at the beginning of such sentences. The nouns qualified by such sentences are always identical with nouns or verbs within the sentences themselves.

6.19 When the noun qualified is identical with the subject of the sentence that is functioning as a qualifier, that subject is replaced by *ó*. For example:

Ọkùnrin tí ó pè mí   (The man who called me),

ó here stands for *ọkùnrin* (a man).

6.20 When the noun qualified is identical with the object of the sentence functioning as a qualifier, that object is dropped completely. For example:

Ọkùnrin tí mo rí   (The man I saw)

The object of the verb *rí* is *ọkùnrin*.

6.21 When the noun qualified is identical with the object of any one of the following prepositions: *fi, ti, bá, fún* and *sí* within the sentence functioning as a qualifier, that object is dropped completely. For example:

Ọ̀bẹ tí mo fi gé e   (The knife that I cut it with)
                (ọ̀bẹ = object of *fi*)
ìlú tí mo ti wá   (The town where I came from)
                (ìlú = object of *ti*)
ẹni tí mo bá rà á   (The person I bought it for)
                (ẹni = object of *bá*)
ẹni tí mo rà á fún   (The person I bought it for)
                (ẹni = object of *fún*)
ibi tí mo jù ú sí   (The place I threw it into)
                (ibi = object of *sí*)

6.22 When the noun qualified is identical with the object of the preposition *ní* within the sentence functioning as a qualifier, several things happen:

(i) the object of the preposition is dropped;
(ii) the preposition is either dropped or placed immediately to the left of the noun qualified;
(iii) if the object dropped was a place noun, the preposition *ti* is placed somewhere to the left of the verb of the sentence functioning as qualifier, unless the verb is *wà* (be in a place) or *gbé* (to reside in), neither of which requires *ti*.

For example:

ní ọjọ́ tí ó dé)
ọjọ́ tí.ó dé)   (The day on which he arrived)
                (ọjọ́=object of *ní*)

95

ní ibi tí mo ti rà á)
    ibi tí mo ti rà á)   (Where I bought it)
            (ibi (place noun)=object of *ní*)
ní ibi tí mo wà)
    ibi tí mo wá)   (Where I was)
    (ibi (place noun)=object of *ní*; verb=*wà*)

6.23 When the noun qualified is identical with the genitival
qualifier of the sentence functioning as a qualifier, the genitival
qualifier is replaced by *rè* for singular items, and *wọn* for
plural ones.   For example:

Ọmọ tí olè jí ìwé rè   (The child whose books were stolen)
            (ọmọ = genitival qualifier)
Àwọn tí olè jì íwé wọn   (Those whose books were stolen)
            (àwọn = genitival qualifier)

6.24 When the noun qualified is derived from the verb of
the sentence functioning as a qualifier, nothing happens.
For example:
    jíjí tí olè jí ìwé ọmọ   (The fact/way that the boy's books
        náà   got stolen)
    The introducer *tí* is said to be a relative pronoun in
traditional grammars of the language. That view is completely rejected here, as the introducer never 'stands for'
any nouns, as pronouns are said to do (on this, see **2.12** above).
Thus, it does not stand for anything at all in the example
given here in the present section.

THE INTRODUCER *ni*

6.25 The introducer *ni* marks sentences that are made to
function as (topical) qualifiers. It always appears at the
beginning of such sentences. The nouns qualified by such
sentences are always identical with nouns or verbs within
the sentences themselves. The changes which the latter nouns
undergo are the same as those mentioned above under
relative clause qualifiers. For this reason, they do not have
to be described under the introducer *ni*.

96

6.26 This word *ni,* contrary to popular English-inspired belief, is an introducer, and not a verb. It is an introducer because its function is the same as that of the introducers discussed earlier. It occurs in exactly the same position as the introducer *tí,* for example. Not only that, *tí* regularly occurs optionally in place of *ni* in sentences that would otherwise have contained more than one occurrence of the latter. For example:

Ìwọ ni mo ń bá sọrọ̀ tí o   (How dare you grumble when
  ń kùn?   I talk to you?)

Since *tí* is not a verb, *ni* cannot be a verb either. (For more on *ni,* see **8.14** below).

6.27 Introducer for Verbs
Elements that are employed as verbs are never marked by any introducers. It is the function of such elements which serves most clearly to indicate that they are verbs. And, as indicated earlier, the only way to form new verbs in the language is to make words from other parts of speech or other languages function as predicator.

6.28 Introducers for Modifiers
As noted earlier in Chapter 5, modifiers are of two kinds—adverbs and adverbials. Adverbs are single words, while adverbials are phrases, i.e. combinations of two words or more.

6.29 Adverbs are not marked by introducers. The number of adverbs in the language is fixed. There is no regular way at all to create new adverbs in the language.

6.30 An adverbial normally consists of an introducer followed by a noun or nominalisation and its qualifier, if any. The introducers that occur in adverbials are traditionally known as prepositions. The prepositions in the language number around seven. They are:

fi	(with, by means of)	ní	(in, at, to, on)
bá	(for, in company with, on behalf of)		
ti	(from)	fún	(for, on behalf of)
sí	(to, in, at)	pèlú	(by)

97

6.31 The Preposition *fi*

This preposition can be used with almost any kind of noun. It forms an adverbial phrase of means or instrument with the nouns that it accompanies.

Ó fi ìbọn pa á. (He killed it with a gun.)

6.32 The Preposition *bá*[1]

This preposition occurs most usually with human nouns. For example:

Ó bá mi rà á bọ̀. (He bought and brought it for me.)

6.33 The Preposition *ti*

This preposition is used only with nouns of place and time, as in:

Mo ti ibẹ̀ dé ní àárọ̀. (I got back from there in the morning.)

Ó ti àárọ̀ bẹ̀rẹ̀ ìṣekúṣe. (He began behaving badly from his youth.)

6.34 The Preposition *sí*

The preposition *sí* occurs with nouns referring to place, time, human beings and animals.

Wọ́n fi ìpàdé náà sí ìrọ̀lẹ́. (The meeting was fixed for the evening.)

Mo lọ sí ọjà. (I went to the market.)

Wọ́n kọ ìwé sí mi. (They wrote to me.)

6.35 The Preposition *ní*

This preposition normally occurs with nouns denoting place, time, manner, or circumstance. For example:

Ó wà ní ilé. (He is at home.)

---

[1] There is a verb *bá* (to overtake) in the language which is distinct both in function and in meaning from this preposition. This is why the sentence *ó bá mi rà á* is ambiguous. In one of its two meanings it contains the preposition *bá*, while in the other it contains the verb *bá* (to overtake, to join, accompany). With *bá* as a preposition, the sentence means 'He bought it for me', whereas with *bá* as a verb, it means 'He bought it from me'.

Ó dé ní àárọ̀.	(He arrived in the morning.)
Wọ́n dá aṣọ náà ní pelebe.	(The garment was made too short.)
Máa lọ ní bí mo ti ń wò	
ẹ́ yìí.	(Get going right now!)

The preposition *ní* never precedes anything that is not a noun or nominalisation in the language. In other words, it is followed directly by nouns/nominalisations only.

6.36 The Preposition *fún*[1]

This preposition is used most commonly with human nouns. For example:

Ó ta iṣu náà fún mi.	(He helped me to sell the yams.)
Ẹ pè é fún mi.	(Call him for me.)

6.37 The Preposition *pẹ̀lú*

This preposition's status is somewhat doubtful. In other words, it may be possible or desirable to call it something else. When used 'correctly', it has the same meaning as *fi* (with, by)

Ó ṣe é pẹ̀lú túláàsì.	(He did it by force.)

6.38 The following elements are no prepositions. They are combinations of prepositions or verbs and object nouns.

nínú	(ní inú)	(inside)
lórí	(ní orí)	(on top of)
lérí	(lé orí)	(on top of)
nípa	(ní ipa)	(about, in connection with)
lábẹ́	(ní abẹ́)	(under)
nítorí	(ní ti orí)	(on account of)
láti	(ní à-ti)	(from)

---

[1]There is a verb *fún* (to give) in the language which is distinct both in meaning and in function from this preposition. This is why the sentence *Ó ta iṣu náà fún mi* is ambiguous. In one of its two meanings it contains the preposition *fún*, while in the other it contains the verb *fún*. With the latter, the sentence means 'He sold the yams to me'.

Even *pèlú* behaves as a combination of a verb and an object noun. This can be seen from the actual pronunciation of the following sentence:

Ó ṣe é pèlúu túlààsì.   (He did it by force.)

Cf. the complex verb *pèlú* in **4·15** above and the conjunction *pélú* in **7·5** and **7·7** below. *Pèlú* also occurs as a sentential; see **5·29** above.

THE 'INTRODUCER' *kó*

6.39 It is convenient to consider under the general heading of introducers the two items *kó* and *ní*.[1]

The item *kó* means (not). It is used to negate nouns only. It follows the nouns that it negates. For example:

Ìwọ kó ni mo pè.   (I didn't call you.)
Bẹ́ẹ̀ kó.   (It is not so.)

THE PARTICLE *ní*

6.40 The item *ní* has no meaning that could be looked up in a dictionary of the language. In this respect, it is different from the following:

ní	(to have)	(Verb)
ní	(to say)	(Verb)
ní	(to help)	(Verb)
ní	(to load a ship)	(Verb)
ní	(in, at)	(Preposition)

The item functions only in sentences with the 'particle' *ní* (see **8.10** and **8.20** below). There it indicates that the

---

[1] This means that these two elements are grouped with introducers proper purely for convenience and not on the basis of actual function, as is the case for other elements. This grouping is convenient from the practical point of view, as the only alternative to it is to recognize each of the two elements as forming a distinct part of speech all by itself, in which case, it would be necessary to write an entire chapter of at most a page for each of them. That would be very wasteful of space, to say the least.

normal order of occurrence of some nouns has been tampered with. Examples of such sentences are:

Ó jí mi ní owó.	(He stole my money.)
Ó ta mi ní ìpá.	(He kicked me.)
Ó jà mí ní iyàn.	(He argued with me.)

COMPREHENSION

1. What are introducers?
2. Name one major part of speech for which there are no introducers at all.
3. What part of speech has the largest number of introducers, and what is the number of such introducers?
4. How are sentences turned into nouns or nominalisations?
5. What introducers occur with parts of sentences (as opposed to whole sentences) that function as nouns?
6. Make a list of all the introducers for qualifiers.
7. What are relative clause qualifiers derived from? What introducer is employed for that purpose?
8. What kinds of nouns occur with the preposition *ní*?
9. What kinds of nouns occur with the prepositions *sí* and *fi*?
10. What work does the 'introducer' *kò* (not) do? In what way is it different from the other introducers?

EXERCISES

A What is the meaning of the introducer *o* exemplified in Section **6.6**?

B Suggest a common meaning for the introducers exemplified in Section **6.7**. Do the same thing for those exemplified in Sections **6.8**, **6.9**, **6.10**, **6.12** and **6.13**.

C Identify the introducers and the other elements combined to form the following: e.g. onílégogoro = o-nílégogoro
                                                 nílégogoro = ní-ilé-gogoro

1. alákọrí	8. ségesège	15. ní ṣíṣèntèlé
2. ìjà	9. àìsùn	16. àsọtélè
3. ìkẹ́fà	10. jíjẹ	17. àbẹ̀kẹ́
4. alùpùpù	11. láti ìjẹta	18. ìmúná
5. òta	12. kúkúrú	19. òjíṣẹ́
6. ọdẹ	13. nítorí	20. alàgbà
7. ìgbàkúùgbà	14. síbèsíbè	

D   *(i)* Three relative clause constructions can be formed from the following sentence:

    Òjó lu Dàda.

One of them is:

    Òjó tí ó lu Dàda

What are the two others?

(ii) In a similar fashion, form relative clause constructions from the following sentences. Use such constructions in sentences:

1. Mo ra ìwé ní ọjà.
2. Ó pa irọ́ fún mi.
3. Ọkọ̀ rẹ̀ wà ní ọdọ̀ mọ́kálíìkì.
4. Ọlọ́pàá mú olè méjì.
5. Ìwé mi wà ní ibẹ̀.

E   *(i)* Three topical qualifier sentence constructions can be formed from the sentence:

    Òjó lu Dàda.

One of them is:

    Òjó ni ó lu Dàda.

What are the two others?

(ii) In a similar fashion, form topical qualifier sentence constructions from the sentences given above in Exercise **E** *(ii)*.

F   Complete the following:

(i) Phrase   *Synonymous Relative Clause construction*

  a igi gíga   igi tí ó ga
  b ẹran gbígbẹ   ....
  c ẹja yínyan   ....
  d aṣọ dúdú   ....
  e omi tútù   ....
  f omi mímu   ....
  g ohun jíjẹ   ....
  h ẹran títà   ....
  i ìlà wíwọ́   ....
  j iṣu sísè   ....
  k ọ̀rọ̀ rẹpẹtẹ ....

(ii) a èèyàn dáadáa   èèyàn tí ó dára
    b ....   ọ̀nà tí ó jìn
    c ....   ìlú tí ó tóbi
    d ....   ẹrù tí ó wúwo.
    e ....   ìyà tí ó pọ̀
    f ....   ọgbọ́n tí ó ṣe ẹ̀wẹ́
    g ....   ọ̀rẹ́ mi tí ó ṣe ọ̀wọ́n
    h ....   ọjà tí ó wọ́n
    i ....   ohun tí ó mú ayọ̀ wá
    j ....   ẹni tí mo mọ̀
    k ....   ilé tí ó ga gogoro

G   Correct the following ungrammatical utterances:

1. Ẹ jẹ́ k'á bẹ̀rẹ̀ ìsìn wa nípa kíkọ orin ọgbọ̀n.
2. Nítorí pé ọ̀nà mọ́tò kò dára, gbogbo èèyàn wá bẹ̀rẹ̀ sí 'íti Ìbàdàn lọ sí Èkó nípa ọkọ̀ rélùweè.
3. Nípa ìfẹ́ olùgbàlà kì yóò sí nǹkan.
4. Wọn ń fi ẹmí wọn wu ewu nípa fífi ẹsẹ̀ rìn wọ agbami.
5. Ǹjẹ́ o mọ orúkọ ọjà tí mo ra ẹ̀wù mi náà?
6. Ṣé ọkùnrin tí olè fọ́ ilé ni?
7. Òjó ni sọ bẹ́ẹ̀.
8. Ó ṣìn kù sí ibi tí mo rà á ní.
9. Ibi tí mo ti jù ú sí ní 'yẹn.
10. Ẹ kú àpalẹ̀mọ́ ọdún o.
11. Àpajẹ ni tòlótòló wà fún.
12. Orin èfẹ̀ yí wà láti bú ènìyàn.

H   Why is it incorrect to call the following words prepositions?

nínú	(inside)	lábẹ́	(under, beneath)
lórí	(on top of)	nítorí	(on account of)
lérí	(on top of)	láti	(from)
nípa	(in connection with)		

Say what items have been combined to form each of them.

103

CHAPTER 7

Conjunctions and Disjunctions

7.1 **Conjunctions** and **disjunctions** are used to indicate the relationship existing between two elements or more. Such a relationship is either one of togetherness or one of separateness.

ACTUAL FUNCTION AND CHARACTERISTICS

7.2 **Conjunctions** show that two or more things go together or are united. For example:

Owó àti ọmọ   (money and children)
Mo fẹ́ owó àti ọmọ.   (I want money and children.)

Disjunctions, on the other hand, show that two elements or more are alternatives, and a person can only choose one of such items. For example:

Owó tàbí ọmọ   (either money or children)
Mo fẹ́ owó tàbí ọmọ.   (I want either money or child-
                                 ren.)

7.3 Conjunctions and disjunctions relate elements of the same functional class. Thus they relate nouns to nouns, adverbials to adverbials, and sentences to sentences. They never relate adverbials to sentences, for example, because adverbials are functionally not the same class of elements as sentences.

7.4 Furthermore, conjunctions and disjunctions normally occur between the two items that they relate. This is so in the two examples above.

CONJUNCTIONS

7.5 Yoruba only has conjunctions for joining nouns or adverbials. In other words, the language has no conjunctions for joining sentences, adverbs or qualifiers.

Conjunctions are only three in number. They are:

ti/àti   (and)   pèlú   (and)   òun   (and)

7.6 The first of these conjunctions, namely, *àti* joins nouns or adverbials. For example:

owó àti àlàáfíà ara	(money and good health)
àtijẹ àti àtimu	(what to eat and what to drink)
ní àárò àti ní alẹ	(in the morning and in the evening)

The following two examples do not mean exactly the same thing. The kinds of things joined together there are not the same.

ní ayé àti ní òrun	(in heaven and on earth)
ní ayé àti òrun	(in heaven and earth)

The elements joined together in the second phrase are not *ní ayé* and *òrun*, but rather *ayé* and *òrun*. After the two elements had been joined together, they were then marked with the preposition *ní* as functioning in an adverbial. In the first phrase, two adverbials are joined together. This phrase is more emphatic than the second.

Each of the elements joined by *àti* can be preceded by this conjunction. For example:

àti owó àti àlàáfíà ara   (money and good health)

Phrases like the one given here sound slightly more emphatic than those having only one occurrence of the conjunction.

Ti, which seems to be a reduced form of *àti*, normally occurs preceding each of the items it joins together, as in:

ti ajá ti ẹran (dogs and goats, i.e. every Tom, Dick and Harry)
ti òsán ti òru (= ti ní òsán ti ní òru) (both day and night)

But in the phrase exemplified in the following sentence, only one occurrence of the conjunction is permissible:

Ó dé ti àìdé ni wón kó ẹjọ́ wá sí iwájú rẹ̀. (He had scarcely arrived there when they brought their disputes to him for arbitration.)

Notice that the phrase *ó dé ti àìdé* is made up of two conjoined nouns/nominalisations, *ó dé* and *àìdé*, functioning together as the object of a deleted preposition *ní*. For this reason, the above sentence has essentially the same structure as:

Àná ni wón kó ẹjọ́ wá sí iwájú rẹ̀. (It was yesterday that they brought their disputes to him for arbitration.)

7.7 The conjunctions *pẹ̀lú* and *òun* join nouns only. For example:

Òjó pẹ̀lú Dàda   (Ojo and Dada)
Òjó òun Dàda   (Ojo and Dada)

DISJUNCTIONS

7.8 The disjunctions in the language are:

àfi/àyàfi	(except, but for, apart from)
àmọ́	(but)
ṣùgbọ́n	(but)
bóyá. . .àbí/tàbí	(whether. . . or)
yálà. . . àbí/tàbí	(or, either. . . . . or)
ańbọ̀ọ̀sì/ańbọ̀tórí/ańbèlèńté	(much less; let alone)

7.9 The disjunction *àfi* (or *àyàfi* for some speakers) is used with nouns and adverbials. For example:

Òkété kì í jáde ní ọ̀sán àfi ní òru. (The giant rat never comes out in the daytime but instead at night only.)

Kò sí ewu ní oko àfi gììrì aparò lásán. (There is no danger on the farm, apart from the noise of partridges taking off.)

The first of the elements related by the disjunction is often left unexpressed. For example:

àfi èyí tí ó tún dé 'lẹ̀ yìí	(but for this new development)
àfi èmi àfi òun	(It's him and me alone, (and no one else).)

7.10 The disjunctions *àmọ́* and *ṣùgbọ́n* are used with sentences only. For example:

Mo wò ó, àmọ́ mi ò mú un.	(I examined it, but I didn't take it.)
Mo rí i, ṣùgbọ́n mi ò kí i.	(I saw him, but I didn't greet him.)

The first of the two sentences related by these disjunctions is often left unexpressed. For example:

àmọ́ ó ti wọ́n jù	(but it's too costly)
ṣùgbọ́n ó ti wọ́n jù	(but it's too costly)

7.11 The disjunction *àbí* (or *tàbí*) is employed with nouns, adverbials and sentences. For example:

Ìgbà wo ni kí n wá, ní àárọ̀ ni tàbí ní alẹ́?	(When should I come, in the morning or in the evening?)
Yan owó tàbí ọmọ.	(Choose either money or children.)
Ó ti dé tàbí kò ì tí ì dé?	(Has he come back or not?)

As in the case of the two sets of disjunctions already considered, the first of the two sentences related by *àbí* or *tàbí* can be left out unexpressed. For example:

Àbí kò níí wá ni?	(Or is it that he doesn't plan to come?)

7.12 The items *yálà* and *bóyá* are normally paired with *tàbí*. They always appear before the first of the two elements related by *tàbí*. When *bóyá* is present, such elements normally are sentences only. This is not so in the case of *yálà*. For example:

Wá yálà ní alẹ́ tàbí ní àárọ̀.	(Come either in the evening or in the morning.)

Yálà òjò rò tàbí kò rò, mo
gbọ́dọ̀ dé'bẹ̀.

(Whether it rains or not, I
must go there.)

Kìkì ohun tí mo fẹ́ 'ẹ́mọ̀ ni
bóyá ó wá tàbí kò wá.

(All I want to know is whether
he came or he didn't.)

7.13 The disjunction *ańbọ̀sì*, (or its variants *ańbọ̀sìbọ́sí*, *ańbọ̀tórí* and *ańbèlèǹté*), is used with nouns and adverbials. The second of the two elements which the disjunction relates always comes last in its sentence. For example:

Kò ní ìyàwó ańbọ̀sì ọmọ.

(He doesn't have a wife, much
less a child.)

Ọkùnrin ò lè ṣe é ańbọ̀sì
obìnrin.

(Men can't do it, much less
women.)

Kì í jẹun ní alẹ́ ańbọ̀sì ní
òru.

(He doesn't eat in the evening,
much less in the night.)

7.14 The table that follows restates in summary form the information given above about the types of elements that conjunctions and disjunctions relate. The minus sign (−) occurs under any element that a particular conjunction or disjunction cannot relate, while the plus sign (+) occurs under those that it can relate.

	SENTENCES	NOUNS	ADVERBIALS
àti/ti	−	+	+
òun	−	+	−
pẹ̀lú	−	+	−
àyàfi/àfi	−	+	+
tàbí/àbí	+	+	+
ańbọ̀sì	−	+	+
ṣùgbọ́n	+	−	−
àmọ́	+	−	−
bóyá . . . . . tàbí	+	−	−
yálà . . . . . tàbí	+	+	+

COMPREHENSION

1. What are conjunctions?
2. What are disjunctions?
3. What do conjunctions and disjunctions have in common?
4. What is the difference between conjunctions and disjunctions?
5. What do conjunctions join?
6. How many conjunctions are there?
7. Do all the conjunctions have the same meaning?
8. How many disjunctions are there? Do they have exactly the same meaning?
9. Do all the disjunctions in Yoruba relate the same kinds of items?
10. What is peculiar about *añbọ̀sì?*

EXERCISES

A Identify the different uses of *pẹ̀lú* in the following sentences:
1. 'Owó wù mí; ayá wù mí pẹ̀lú.'
2. Èyí pẹ̀lú àwọn ohun tí ó mú kí n wá.
3. Òun pẹ̀lú Dàda ni mo rí ní 'bẹ̀.
4. Ó ṣe iṣẹ́ náà pẹ̀lú túláàsì.
5. Kí Ọlọ́run wà pẹ̀lú ẹ.

B First determine what is grammatically wrong with the following utterances, and then make corrections as necessary.
1. Inú wa dùn pé wọn kò fi ara jó'ná tàbí fi ara pa.
2. Ó ní bí wọ́n bá sọ̀rọ̀ tàbí pa ariwo, ojú wọn yóò rí nǹkan.
3. Oko kì í ṣe 'élọ yálà fún àwọn eléégún àti awọn èro t'ó wá wò'ran.
4. Wọ́n tún lè bẹ̀rẹ̀ sí 'íja 'lè àti ṣe ohun búburú mìíràn.
5. Bí wọ́n bá fẹ́ nǹkànkan, wọn á lọ sí ọdọ̀ Ṣàngó, wọn á sì jẹ́ ẹ̀jẹ́ pẹ̀lú rẹ̀.
6. Àgbà añbọ̀sì ọmọdé kò lè dá orí erin gbé.
7. Àwọn ènìyàn yóò máa ṣe ìyẹ́sí wọn pẹ̀lú owó àti oníruurú ẹ̀bùn.
8. Òkété kì í jáde ní ọsán áfi òru.
9. Ó tóbi, àfi àwọ̀ rẹ̀ kò wù mí.
10. Èyí t'ó wà ní'bí ṣùgbọ́n ìyẹn kò dára.

C *(i)* If you study Chapters 5 and 7 carefully enough, you will find at least three reasons why *sì* has not been analysed as a conjunction in this book. What are those three reasons?

(ii) Can you think of any more compelling reasons why that same item should on the contrary have been analysed as a conjunction for joining sentences, as it is popularly believed to be?

D The item *pèlú* as in Exercise **A**1 above is analysed as a Sentential in this book (see Section **5.29** above). Should it have been analysed as a conjunction for joining sentences? Justify your answer.

CHAPTER 8

Sentences

8.1 Basic Word Order

The parts of speech or word classes discussed in the preceding six chapters have particular places or sets of places in which they normally occur within sentences. On the basis of this, one can talk of the normal or basic word order in Yoruba sentences.

8.2 Subject, Object, Predicator

The normal order of occurrence for subject, predicator and object is:

| Subject | Predicator | Object |

For example:

Òjó ra mótò.   (Ojo bought a vehicle.)

Here, *Òjó* is subject, *rà* is predicator, and *mótò* is object.

8.3 Qualifiers

A subject or an object may consist of just a noun or of a noun and its qualifier(s). When a qualifier is present, it always follows the noun it qualifies. For example:

Òjó náà ra mótò tuntun.   (Ojo, too, bought a new vehicle.)

Here *náà* and *tuntun* are qualifiers.

8.4 Sententials

Sententials occur either at the very beginning or at the end of sentences. For example:

Ǹjẹ́ Òjó náà ra mótò tuntun?   (Did Ojo, too, buy a new vehicle?)

Òjó náà ra mótò tuntun bí?   (Did Ojo, too, buy a new vehicle?)

Here *Ǹjẹ́* and *bí* are sententials.

8.5 Adverbs and Adverbials

Adverbs and adverbials occur *(i)* between subject and predicator, *(ii)* after predicator, when no object is present, and *(iii)* after object.

When they occur between subject and predicator, adverbs and adverbials appear in the order:

Adverb   Adverbial

For example:

Òjó náà lè bá mi ra mọ́tò (Ojo, too, can help me buy a
tuntun.   new vehicle.)

Here, *lè* is an adverb, and *bá mi* an adverbial.

When they occur after predicator or object, they appear in the order:

Adverbial   Adverb[1]

For example:

Òjó náà ra mọ́tò tuntun (Ojo, too, bought a new vehicle
ní ibẹ̀ rí.   there before.)

8.6 But it should be remembered that only a class of adverbs and adverbials can occur between subject and predicator, while another class of adverbs and adverbials similarly can only occur after predicator or object. The same thing is true of some sententials. Some occur only at the beginning of sentences, others only at the end of sentences, and still others either at the beginning or at the end of sentences.

---

[1]The reverse order, namely, adverb adverbial, has to be followed, or is at least preferred, for some utterances, however. For example:

Mo gbádùn rẹ̀ gan-an ní àná.   (I thoroughly enjoyed it yesterday.)
Mi ò rí i mọ́ ní àti ìgbà yẹn. (I haven't seen him again since then.)

8.7 The diagram given below summarizes the normal order of words in Yoruba sentences.

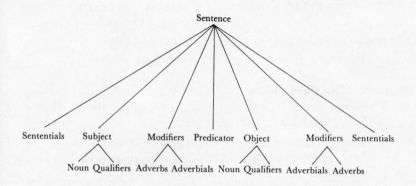

NON-BASIC WORD ORDER

8.8 Under certain circumstances, words appearing in the orders described above can be re-arranged. The orders produced by such re-arrangement are non-basic.

8.9 Relative/Topical Qualifier Formation
Changes in word order invariably occur when relative clause qualifiers and topical qualifiers are formed. Such changes involve (1) subject, (2) object (of verb or preposition), and (3) genitival qualifier.

When these two qualifiers are formed, object always gets moved from its normal place of occurrence. For example:

Ìwé tí mo rà   (the book that I bought)
Ìwé ni mo rà.   (It was a book that I bought.)

Here, *ìwé* (book) is the object of *rà*. Under normal circumstances, *ìwé* would occur right after *rà*.

Subject and genitival qualifier get moved also, though replacements are left in their original positions. For example:

Òjó ni ó jí owó Dàda.   (It was Ojo that stole Dada's money.)

Dàda ni Òjó jí owó rè.   (Dada is the person whose money Ojo stole.)

Here *Òjó* is subject, and *Dàda* genitival qualifier.

For more on topical qualifiers, see **8.31** below.

8.10 The Particle *ní*

The word order in any expression containing the particle *ní* is always nonbasic. For example:

Òjó jí Dàda ní owó.   (Ojo stole Dada's money.)

Òjó ja Dàda ní iyàn.   (Ojo argued with Dada.)

In the first of these examples, *Dàda* is a genitival qualifier, and in the second, it is an object. This can be seen in the following equivalent or variant sentences with basic word order:

Òjó jí owó Dàda.   (Ojo stole Dada's money.)

Òjó bá Dàda ja iyàn.   (Ojo argued with Dada.)

For more on sentences like these, see **8.20** below.

8.11 The Disjunction *ańbòsì*

One half of the subject always gets moved to the end of the sentence when the disjunction *ańbòsì* relates elements functioning as subject. For example:

Okùnrin ò lè se é, ańbòsì   (Men can't do it, much less obìnrin.   women.)

Here *okùnrin* and *obìnrin* function jointly as the subject of the verb *se*. This is the only word order permitted in sentences like the one given here.

VERBS AND SENTENCES

8.12   Verbs play a central role in sentences. For while other parts of speech may be absent from sentences, verbs are almost always present there.

8.13 Imperative Sentences

These are sentences employed for giving orders, directions, instructions, etc. Such sentences may consist of one word only. Such a word is almost always a verb. Example:

> lọ (go!)
> wá (come here!)

Imperative sentences addressed to single individuals normally do not have subjects. For example:

> Kúrò ní ibẹ̀. (Get away from there!)

However, when emphasis is desired, the subject may be specified. That subject is always *ìwọ*. For example:

> Ìwọ, kúrò ní ibẹ̀ yẹn! (You, get away from that place!)

Imperative sentences addressed to groups of individuals always have their subject specified. The subject normally is the noun *ẹ*. For example:

> Ẹ kúrò ní ibẹ̀ yẹn! (You people, get away from there!)

Imperative sentences addressed to single individuals can occur with *ẹ* as their subject. This happens when the aim is to show respect for the person being addressed.

> Ẹ jókòó sí ibí. (Sit down here, Sir!)

There are some verbs which are employed almost exclusively in imperative sentences only. They are *kú, pẹ̀lẹ́/ńlẹ́/wẹ̀ẹ́* and *jòwọ́/jọ̀ọ́*.

> Ẹ kú ⎫
> Ẹ pẹ̀lẹ́ ⎬ (Types of greeting)
> Ẹ jọ̀ọ́! (Please!)

8.14 Sentences with unspecified Verbs

There are two kinds of sentences in which verbs can be left out unspecified. The first is:

> Ìyẹn iní (ení). (That makes one.)
> Ìyàwó mi ni. (She is my wife.)
> Ta ni ìyẹn? (Who is that?)

The word *ni* is not a verb in these sentences. The verb that has been left out unspecified is either *jẹ́* (to be) or *ṣe* (to be). This is because these sentences have the same meanings as:

Ìyẹn jẹ́ iní (ení).　　　(That makes one.)

Ìyàwó mi ni ó jẹ́. 　} 　(She is my wife.)
Ìyàwó mi ni ó ń ṣe. 　}

Ta ni ìyẹn jẹ́/Ta ni ìyẹn
ń ṣe?　　　　　　　　(Who is that?)

The other type of sentence in which the verb may be unspecified is:

Ẹ tètè!　　　　　　　(Hurry up!)

This sentence cannot be used unless it is already clear from the (situational) context what verb has been left out. Such a verb normally represents some form of activity. Two other sentences like this are:

Ó ṣe é, ṣùgbọ́n kò mọ̀ọ́nmọ̀.　(He did it, but not intention-
　　　　　　　　　　　　ally.)
Kò dédé tí ẹ fi rí mi.　　(I haven't come here without
　　　　　　　　　　　　a reason.)

8.15　Verbs play a central role in sentences in yet another way. They help to differentiate many types of sentences from one another.

8.16　Serial Verbal Sentences

These are sentences containing serial verbs. They are always complex, because each of them always contains at least two verbs. For example:

Ó jí ẹran jẹ.　　　　　(He stole some meat and ate it.)

Serial verbal sentences are formed by combining parts of simple sentences. Thus, the example given above was formed by combining the following two simple sentences:

Ó jí ẹran.　　　　　　(He stole meat.)
Ó jẹ ẹran.　　　　　　(He ate meat.)

　The order in which verbs occur in serial verbal sentences is significant. In some cases, a reversal of that order brings about a change in meaning. For example:

Ó lọ ra ẹran.	(He/She went to buy meat.)
Ó ra ẹran lọ.	(He/She bought some meat and took it along with him/her.)

In other cases, a reversal of the order produces nonsensical utterances. For example:

Ó ra ẹran tà.	(He/She bought meat for re-sale.)
Ó ta ẹran rà.	(Meaningless?)
Ó ra ẹran jẹ.	(He/She bought meat and ate it.)
Ó jẹ ẹran rà.	(Senseless)

Simple independent sentences are sometimes used instead of serial verbal sentences, apparently for emphasis. Thus, people sometimes say:

Ó burú. Ó ju èpè.	(It is bad. It is more than a curse.)

instead of the normal or more usual:

Ó burú ju èpè.	(It is worse than a curse.)

Serial verbal sentences constitute a very important and very common construction in the language. Failure to employ it where it would normally be expected may give the speaker away as a beginner.

8.17 Splitting Verb Sentences

Such sentences contain splitting verbs. These verbs always split in two. One half occurs before the object, and the other after it. For example:

Ó ba ìwé náà jẹ́.	(He damaged the book.)

Splitting verb sentences look and sound like serial verbal sentences. But the two types of sentences are, in fact, different. Splitting verb sentences are in the majority of cases idiomatic in meaning. Partly for this reason, they are not formed by combining simple sentences.

To see this, consider the following serial verbal sentence given earlier:

Ó jí ẹran jẹ.	(He stole some meat and ate it.)

It has the same meaning as:

Ó jí ẹran. Ó jẹ ẹ́.	(He stole some meat. He ate it.)

Therefore, we can say that it was formed by combining appropriate parts of these latter two simple sentences.

The following splitting verb sentence, by contrast,

Ó tàn mí jẹ.   (He deceived me.)

does not mean the same thing as these two simple sentences put together.

Ó tàn mí.   *Ó jẹ mí.

(As a matter of fact, one of the two simple sentences is meaningless in the present context). For this reason, we have to say that it was not formed by combining any simple sentences. This means that it is itself a simple sentence. The same thing holds true for all the other splitting verb sentences in the language.

8.18 Echoing Verb Sentences
The type of sentences referred to by this term can be exemplified by the following:

Ó dá mi dá iṣẹ́ náà.   (He left me alone to do the job.)

Not much is known at present about how such sentences are formed. They seem to be related to serial verbal sentences. However, their meanings, unlike the meanings of serial verbal sentences, are often slightly idiomatic.   For example:

Rò mí ro ire.   (Wish me well.)

8.19 Nominal Assimilating Verb Sentences
These are sentences containing nominal assimilating verbs. For example:

Ó ṣòro 'óṣe.   (It is difficult to do.)

Every sentence in this group can be said in many different ways, without any difference in meaning. Thus, the example given above also occurs as:

Ó ṣòro 'íṣe
Ó ṣòro ṣíṣe
Ó ṣòro ní 'íṣe   (It is difficult to do.)
Ó ṣòro ní ṣíṣe
Ó ṣòro ní àtiṣe

The first three of these examples and the one given earlier are all derived from the fourth; that is from:

Ó ṣòro ní ṣíṣe.

8.20 Sentences with the Particle *ní*

As indicated earlier, the word order in sentences with the particle *ní* is non-basic. The particle *ní* seems to occur in such sentences solely as a reminder of this fact. An example of the kind of sentence being referred to is:

Ó jí mi ní owó.   (He stole my money.)

which means the same thing as:

Ó jí owó mi.   (He stole my money.)

Another way of saying the following sentence:

Ó ṣá mi ní àdá.   (He inflicted a cutlass wound on me.)

is:

Ó fi àdá ṣá mi.   (He inflicted a cutlass wound on me.)

Generally speaking, sentences with the particle *ní* sound more elegant than synonymous sentences without it.

8.21 Sentences with Report Verbs

Sentences with report verbs are used for reporting thoughts, observations, news, orders and requests. Such reported thoughts, observations, etc., are normally introduced by the introducer *pé* (that) in the case of thoughts and observations.

For example:

Ó sọ pé òjò rò.   (He said that rain fell.)
Mo mò pé òjò rò.   (I know that rain fell.)

Reported orders, wishes and requests are introduced by the introducer *kí* or *pékí*. For example:

Ó ní kí a wá.   (He asked us to come.)
Ó sọ pé kí a wá.   (He asked us to come.)

In all sentences with report verbs, the phrases (more accurately nominalisations) beginning with the introducers *pé*, *kí*, and *pékí* always function as part of adverbials. However, the preposition *ní* which introduces such adverbials is always left out. But even so such phrases must nevertheless be analysed as part of adverbials. Two reasons were given in **4.19** above, why this is so. For yet another reason, consider the following sentences:

(a)	Ó gba kí o lọ.	(It requires that you go.)
(b)	Ó gbà kí o lọ.	(He agrees that you should go.)
(a)	Ó mọ 'kíákíá'	(He knows the word 'kíákíá'.)
(b)	Ó mọ̀ kíákíá.	(He quickly found out.)
(c)	Ó mọ̀ ní kíákíá.	(He quickly found out.)
(b)	Ó rìn 'hòhò.	(He went nude.)
(c)	Ó rìn ní ìhòhò.	(He went nude.)
(b)	Ó mọ̀ tòótọ́.	(He actually knows.)
(c)	Ó mọ̀ ní tòótọ́.	(He actually knows.)

All the sentences numbered *(a)* are structurally alike. Notice that they contain low-tone verbs whose tone has been changed to mid tone. The sentences numbered *(b)* are also structurally alike: they contain low-tone verbs whose tone is unchanged. The sentences numbered *(c)* are structurally alike, too: they contain the preposition *ní*, and their verbs retain their low tone.

Standard practice in grammar requires that sentences which are structurally alike be analysed in exactly the same way. This means that, as far as the sentences under consideration are concerned, those of them numbered *(a)* above must be analysed in exactly the same way. Similarly for those numbered *(b)* and for those numbered *(c)*.

Now, the last three sentences numbered *(b)* are to be analysed as the shortened or reduced forms of their respective *(c)* variants. This being the case, the first sentence numbered *(b)* must also be analysed as the reduced form of:

(c) Ó gbà ní kí o lọ. (He agrees that you should go.)

where *ní kí o lọ* is an adverbial introduced by the preposition *ní*.

The only difference between this *(c)* sentence and the other *(c)* sentences above is that the preposition *ní* in the latter can be retained while the one in the former apparently cannot, in the existing standard form of the language.

8.22 Sentences with Impersonal Verbs

The subject of the sentences in this category is always ó. It never refers to any person or even thing. In other words, it is impersonal. For example:

Ó dára pé o tètè dé.   (It is good that you returned in good time.)

Kò bọ́ sí i pé o ò lọ.   (It was an error of judgment for you not to have gone.)

As in the case of sentences with report verbs, the phrases beginning with *pé* or *kí* or *pékí* in sentences with impersonal verbs function there as parts of adverbial phrases that have lost their preposition *ní*.

Many, but not all, sentences with impersonal verbs can be said in another way, without any change in their meanings. For example, the two sentences given above also occur as:

Pé o tètè de dára.   (It is good that you returned in good time.)

Pé o ò lọ kò bọ́ sí i.   (It was an error of judgment for you not to have gone.)

In these sentences, the phrases beginning with *pé* function as subject. As such, they replace the impersonal subject *ó* which occurs in the pair of examples first given.

8.23 Sentences with Symmetrical Verbs

Almost all such sentences in the language were given earlier under symmetrical verbs. They are mentioned here again for two reasons. Firstly, so as to stress the fact that they are sentences whose subjects and objects are freely interchangeable. That is no change in meaning occurs when such subjects and objects are interchanged. For example:

Ẹ̀rù bà mí.   }
Mo ba ẹ̀rù.   }   (I was afraid.)

Secondly, to point out that there are many sentences which look deceptively like sentences with symmetrical verbs, but which are in fact not sentences with such verbs. Examples are:

Ikú ń dẹ Dẹ̀dẹ̀.   (Death wants to trap Dẹ̀dẹ̀.)

Dẹ̀dẹ̀ ń dẹ ikú.   (Dẹ̀dẹ̀ wants to trap death.)

Títí wù mí.	(I have taken a fancy to Titi.)
Mo wu Títí.	(Titi has taken a fancy to me.)
Òjó lù mí.	(Ojo hit me.)
Mo lu Òjó.	(I hit Ojo.)

Each member of these pairs of sentences is different in meaning from the other member of the same pair. This would not be the case if these were sentences with symmetrical verbs. Furthermore, the first member of each pair does not imply the second member of the same pair. Again, this would not be the case if the above sentences contained symmetrical verbs.

8.24 Sentences with Causative Verbs

As said earlier in 4.21, there are apparently only five causative verbs in the language. Although they all have the same meaning, *viz* 'to cause', they cannot all be used interchangeably in the following sentences (given earlier) in standard Yoruba.

Ó mú mi şe bẹ́ẹ̀.	(He made me do so.)
Ó fi/mú/dá èrín pa mí.	(He made me laugh.)
Wón sọ ó di ògá.	(They made him a master.)
Ó fi ìyà jẹ mí.	(He punished me.)
Ó dá(?)/şe ikú pa òrẹ́ rẹ̀.	(He brought about his friend's death.)
Ó fi/dá ẹrù pa ọkò.	(He weighed down the vehicle.)

The structure of causative sentences is not simple, since they always contain at least two verbs. The first of the verbs is always the causative verb. The noun following it is its object.

The first sentence above is an altered version of the sentence:

Ó mú kí n şe bẹ́ẹ̀.	(He made me do so.)

In this sentence, *n* (I) is a subject noun. It is the form *mo* (I) takes after the introducer *kí*.

The remaining four sentences have versions like the one just given, but those versions do not seem to occur in current usage, as the one above does. Nevertheless, it is convenient to regard those four causative verb sentences as the altered versions of their respective non-occurring (?) counterparts.

The expression *kí ng ṣe bệệ* in the above sentence is a noun or nominalisation functioning as the object of the causative verb *mú*. The non-occurring counterparts of the last four causative verb sentences above contain similar nouns or nominalisations also.

8.25 Interrogative Sentences

These are sentences that are employed as questions. They are of two basic kinds. One type of interrogative sentences contains question words, the other does not.

Some members of each of the four major parts of speech in the language have interrogative meanings. They are, therefore, used in questions only. Among the nouns, *ta, kí, èwo, èló* and *mélòó* occur in interrogative sentences only. For example:

Ta ni ìyẹn?	(Who is that?)
Kí ni ìyẹn?	(What is that?)
Èwo ni ìyẹn?	(Which one is that?)
Èló ni ìyẹn?	(How much is that?)
Mélòó ni ìyẹn?	(How many are there?)

Among the qualifiers, *ta, kí, èwo, èló* and *mélòó* occur in interrogative sentences only. For example:

Ìwé ta ni ìyẹn?	(Whose book is that?)
Owó kí ni ìyẹn?)	(What is that money for?)
Ìwé wo ni o fẹ́?	(Which book do you want?)
Ẹran èló ni o rà?	(How much worth of meat did you buy?)
Ìwé mélòó ni o rà?	(How many books did you buy?)

Among the verbs, *dà* and *ńkọ́* occur in interrogative sentences only. For example:

Owó náà dà?	(Where is the money?)
Ìwé náà ńkọ́?	(Where is the book?)

Finally, among the modifiers, *ṣé, ǹjẹ́* and *bí* occur in questions only. For example:

Ṣé Òjó lọ?	(Did Ojo go?)
Ǹjẹ́ Òjó lọ?	(Did Ojo go?)
Òjó lọ bí?	(Did Ojo go?)

Interrogative sentences without question words are pronounced specially. The voice is lighter and higher for such sentences than for their declarative versions. Furthermore, such interrogative sentences are often pronounced with raised eyebrows. This raising of the eyebrows helps to identify such sentences as definitely interrogative. Thus, if:

Ó ti lọ.

is pronounced as just described, it will be interpreted as an interrogative sentence meaning (Has he gone?). But if it is not pronounced in that way, the interpretation will be that it is a declarative sentence meaning (He has gone).

8.26 Sentences with Cognate Objects
A cognate object is an object noun derived from the very verb for which it functions as object. For example, the noun *àlá* in this sentence:

Mo lá àlá. (I had a dream.)

Other examples of cognate objects are *ijó, ayọ̀, ìrìn* and *ẹ̀kọ́* in the following sentences:

Ó jó ìjó sákárà. (He danced to sakara music.)
Ó yọ ayọ̀ ńlá. (He rejoiced a great deal.)
Ó rin ìrìn ọlọ́lá. (He walked like a noble person.)
Ó ń kọ́ ẹ̀kọ́. (He is studying.)

There is another type of cognate objects in the language. Such objects are derived from verbs with the introducer *Cí*. The capital letter *C* in this introducer stands for any consonantal sound that begins a verb. The cognate object derived from *lọ* (to go) with this introducer is *lílọ*, and the one derived from *dùn* (to be sweet) is *dídùn*. The use of *lílọ* and *dídùn* as cognate objects can be exemplified by:

Ó lọ lílọ tí kò rò tẹ́lẹ̀. (He made an unplanned trip.)
Ó dun dídùn oyin. (It tastes sweet like honey.)
Ó rọ rírọ̀ ẹ̀kọ. (It feels soft like ẹkọ.)

In these sentences, *lílọ* together with its qualifier is the object of *lọ, dídùn,* also with its own qualifier, is the object of *dùn,* while *rírọ̀ ẹ̀kọ* functions as the object of *rọ̀.* Almost every simple verb (having only one syllable) in the language functions is sentences with cognate objects. Cf. **4.8** above.

8.27 Sentences with Cognate Adverbials

The sentences in this category contain cognate nouns, like the sentences described above. But the cognate nouns in this present category of sentences, unlike those in the sentences already discussed, function within adverbial phrases. Such adverbial phrases contain the preposition *ní*. For example:

Kò lọ ní lílọ.	(He did not go at all.)
Kó dùn ní dìdún.	(It is not sweet at all.)

The preposition *ní* is generally dropped from the more usual forms of such sentences. When that happens, the sentences themselves are then actually pronounced in this way:

Kò lọ 'ọ́lọ.	(He did not go at all.)
Kò dùn 'úndùn.	(It is not sweet at all.)

Sentences with cognate adverbials usually occur in the negative. However, there are affirmative sentences like the following, which in some way recall sentences with cognate adverbials:

Ó lọ ní ti lílọ.	(As far as going is concerned, yes, he went.)
Ó dùn ní ti dídùn.	(As far as sweetness is concerned, yes, it is sweet.)

It does not appear that anything can be dropped from these positive sentences.

8.28 Negative Sentences

There are several kinds of negative sentences in the language. Every such sentence contains at least one negative word. For present purposes, negative words come from the classes of verbs, introducers and modifiers.

The verb *ti* means (to be impossible, find to be impossible). The sentences in which it occurs are here considered as negative. Examples are:

Ó tì.	(No!)
Ikú gbé mi, ó tì mí.[1]	(Death tried me and found me invincible.)
Àlejò oṣù mẹ́sàn-án kì í bá 'ni k'á tì í ṣe.	(It is inconceivable for someone not to be able to properly entertain a guest who gave nine months' advance notice.)
A ò níí ṣe é tì, a ò níí tì í ṣe!	(May we not find it impossible to do.)
A gbé e tì.	(We could not lift it up.)

The introducer *kọ́* (not) is negative in meaning. It negates nouns only, and it always follows the nouns that it negates. More usually, the introducer itself is in turn directly followed by a topical qualifier. Examples of the sentences in which this introducer occurs are:

Èmi kọ́.	(I wasn't the one.)
Iyẹ̀n kọ́ ni a wí.	(That's not what we said.)
Ìwé kọ́ ni mo rà.	(A book wasn't what I bought.)
Ọ̀rọ̀ 'jọ̀ọ́, bá mi ṣe é' kọ́ ni eléyìí.	(Begging wouldn't help in this matter.)

The modifiers (pre-verbal adverbs) *kò, máà/má* and *ì* give negative meanings to the sentences in which they occur. More specifically, they negate the verbs or verb phrases in such sentences.

The adverb *kò* also occurs as *kì, ò, ì, ẹ̀, ọ̀n* and *à*. For example:

Òjó kò lọ.	(Ojo didn't go.)
Òjó ò lọ.	(Ojo didn't go.)
Mi ì lọ.	(I didn't go.)
Ẹ ẹ̀ lọ.	(You didn't go.)
Wọn ọ̀n lọ.	(They didn't go.)
A à lọ.	(We didn't go.)
Kì ń lọ.	(He never goes.)

---

[1] Adeagbo Akinjogbìn, *Ewì Ìwòyí*, Glasgow: W. Collins, Sons and Co. Ltd., 1969, p. 89, line 278; see line 280 also.

Only the full form, *kò* or *kì*, is allowed in sentences from which *ó* (he, she, it) has been dropped (see **2.21** above.) Example:

Kò lọ.　　　　　　(He didn't go.)
Kì í lọ.　　　　　　(He never goes.)

The adverb *máà/má* can be exemplified by:

Máà/Má lọ mọ́.　　　(Don't ever go (there) again.)
Mo lè máà lọ.　　　　(I may/can refuse to go.)

The adverb *i* indicates that something has not happened or did not happen.　For example:

Ì bá lọ.　　　　　　(He would have gone.)

This sentence indicates that the individual concerned would have liked or had to go, but that he actually did not go.

Ó ì lọ bí?　　　　　(Has he gone yet?)[1]

In this sentence, the speaker assumes that the individual concerned has not gone. However, he is not very sure, and he, therefore, wants someone to confirm or disconfirm his assumption.

Mo lè ṣe àìdé 'bẹ̀.　　(I may not get there.)

In this sentence, *àìdé'bẹ̀* (not getting there) is an object noun formed with the introducer *à-* from the verb phrase *ì dé ibẹ̀*.

Two negative adverbs can occur within the same sentence. Normally, when this happen, the two negatives cancel each other out. Consequently, the meaning of the sentence in which such two negative adverbs occur is positive, and not negative.　For example:

Mi ò lè ṣe àìdé 'bẹ̀.　(I always go there/I'll go there,
　　　　　　　　　　no matter what happens.)
Kò lè máà/má wá.　　(He will definitely come.)

For some unknown reason, however, sentences like the following, with two negatives in them, are negative in meaning, not positive.

Ó lè ṣe àìmáà/má wá.　(He may not show up.)

---

[1] This sentence should not be confused with:
　　Ó ṣì lọ bí?　　　　(Did he go still?)

In this sentence, *àìmáà/má wá* (not coming) is an object noun formed with the introducer *à-* from the verb phrase *ì máà wá* with two negative adverbs.

Another sentence like the above is the following in which *kò* and *kì* occur together.

Kò kì ń lọ.   (He doesn't go.)

But this type of sentence is considered by many people as bad, i.e. unacceptable.

8.29   Conditional Sentences

There are always two parts to every conditional sentence. One part is the sentence itself, and the other the sentential modifying it.   For example:

Bí kò bá wá, kò níí rí mi.   (If he does not come, he won't
                                 see me.)

The sentential in this example is *bí kò bá wá* (if he does not come).

The sententials in conditional sentences can either follow or precede the sentence they modify. Such sententials are nominalisations functioning in adverbial phrases from which the preposition *ní* has been dropped. It is in such adverbial phrases that conditions are actually expressed.   For example:

Kò níí rí mi, bí kò bá   (He won't see me, if he doesn't
wá.   come.)

There are two main types of conditional sentences. They are those that talk about events that have already happened, and those that talk about events that are yet to happen.

Conditional sentences that talk about events that are yet to happen usually contain sententials beginning with either the introducer *tí* or the introducer *bí*. Such sententials usually contain the adverb *bá* also.   For example:

Tí kò bá wá, wá 'ásọ   (Report to me if he doesn't
fún mi.   come.)

The introducers *tí* and *bí*, and the adverb *bá* can sometimes be dropped from this first type of conditional sentences. For example:

Bí o fẹ́, bí o kọ̀, wà á lọ. ⎱   (You are going to go, whether
O fẹ́, o kọ̀, wà á lọ.   ⎰   you like it or not.)

Conditional sentences under this category are very easy to confuse with sentences like the following whose sententials specify time rather than condition:

Tí ó bá dé, á á mú ìkan.   (When he arrives, he will take one.)

Sententials which specify time contain the introducer *tí* only. And this *tí* can be preceded by *ìgbà* (time) or *ní ìgbà* (at time). This is not possible for sententials which specify conditions. The last example also occurs as:

Ìgbà tí ó bá dé, á á mú
ìkan.   (When he arrives, he will take
Ní ìgbà tí ó bá dé, á á   one.)
mú ìkan.

Conditional sentences that talk about events that have already happened contain sententials that either begin with the introducer *kí* or begin with no introducer at all. For example:

Kì á ní mo mọ̀, n̄ bá lọ.	(If I had known, I would have gone.)
À bá ní mo mọ̀, n̄ bá lọ.	(Had I known, I would have gone.)
Kí á ní mo mọ̀, n̄ bá ti lọ.	(Had I known, I would have gone already.)
À bá ní mo mọ̀, n̄ bá ti lọ	
Kí á ní mo mọ̀, n kì bá lọ rárá.[1]	(Had I known, I would not have gone at all.)
À bá ní mo mọ̀, n kì bá ti lọ rárá.[1]	(Had I known, I would not have already gone.)
Kí á ní mo mọ̀, n kì bá tí ì lọ.	(Had I known, I wouldn't have gone yet.)

The sententials in this category of conditional sentences always specify conditions which should have been true, but which were actually not true. For this reason, such conditional sentences always carry a tinge of regret.

---

[1] In some dialects, these are said as:
Kí a ní mo mọ̀, n̄ bá tí lọ.   (Had I known, I would not have gone.)

8.30 Timeless Sentences

These are sentences like the following, given earlier in **4.7** above:

Èjì dín l'ógún. (lit. two be-short-of twenty, i.e. 'eighteen')

Òjò pa wèrèpè di ẹni àkọlù. (Rain renders the cow-itch harmless.)

Èèyàn gbé òkèèrè ní 'yì. (Distance usually confers an aura of respectability on people.)

Ẹ̀wọ̀n já ní 'bi ó wù ú. (The chain breaks/snaps wherever it pleases.)

As pointed out then, most (but not all) sentences like these are proverbial or aphoristic in nature. The actions referred to in them are never located in any particular time, which is why such sentences themselves have been described as timeless.

It seems possible to attribute their timelessness to the fact that they lack the high-tone syllable which, as suggested earlier, is probably best interpreted as the present/past action marker (adverb) in the language.

Timeless sentences apparently cannot be interpreted as imperative sentences, since their meanings do not suggest that they are commands. For example, the following sentence lacks the high-tone syllable, but it is clearly recognizable as an imperative sentence both by its actual form and by its meaning:

Èṣù ṣe ọmọ ẹnìkan kí ó fi Ṣàngó ṣe 'ré. (Let some devil-inspired individual dare to ridicule Ṣango.)

Timeless sentences also should not be identified with conditional sentences, because they lack the characteristic two-part structure of the latter. The kind of sentences they are most similar to would seem to be the ones named serial verbal sentences in **8.16** above. But even so, this similarity is only partial. For apart from lacking the high-tone syllable, which serial verbal sentences always have (barring the exceptions noted in **5.11**), timeless sentences apparently cannot be constructed as freely as serial verbal sentences can.

It should be clear from the foregoing that timeless sentences cannot at present be identified with complete confidence.

8.31 Sentences with Topical Qualifiers

As pointed out in **3.16** above, topical qualifiers, unlike the other kinds of qualifiers in the language, can combine with nouns/nominalisations to form sentences. It follows from what was said in **8.9** above, that such sentences display non-basic word order, except in:

Jíjí ni olè jí ìwé ọmọ náà.   (The fact is/was that the boy's book got stolen. Cf. **6.24** above.)

In this sentence, every word is in its right or proper place.

Sentences with topical qualifiers are thought to be 'emphatic' in meaning. This is due to the simple fact that particular words in them have been differentiated from or contrasted with all other comparable words of the same part of speech. Thus, the above example is used to separate the verb *jí* (to steal) from all other verbs that could be used with the noun phrase *ìwé ọmọ náà*, e.g. *ya* (to tear), *yá* (to borrow), *jó* (to burn), *tẹ̀* (to step upon), *sọnù* (to lose), *wò* (to look at), etc.

Sentences with topical qualifiers are extremely common in the language. Failure to employ them in some contexts may give the speaker away as a beginner. Thus the sentence:

Ó jẹ́ ọ̀gá mi.   (He is my boss.)

is perfectly grammatical, but native speakers would most normally say the same thing using a sentence with a topical qualifier, as in:

Ọ̀gá mi ni (ó jẹ́).   (He is my boss.)
Ọ̀gá ni ó jẹ́ fún mi.   (He is my boss.)

The interrogative nouns in the language (see **2.22** above), are employed most normally in sentences with topical qualifiers. Similarly for noun phrases like *ó dé ti àìdé* (he had scarcely arrived) (see **3.4, 6.4** and **7.6** above).

A noun can have more than one topical qualifier qualifying it. Put another way, a sentence can contain strings of two or more consecutive topical qualifiers. For example:

Bàbá ni ó ra bàtà ní Èkó ni ó sáré wá 'lé ni ó kó wọn fún Òjó.   (It was father that bought shoes in Lagos and came home quickly and gave them to Ojo.)

This sentence contains three topical qualifiers; that is, the noun *Bàbá* is qualified by a string of three topical qualifiers.

As indicated earlier (see **6.26** above), all but the first in any such string of topical qualifiers can always be replaced by relative clause qualifiers without much difference in meaning, if any at all, as seen in:

Bàbá ni ó ra bàtà ní Èkó   (It was father that bought shoes
    tí ó sáré wá 'lé tí ó kó   in Lagos and came home quick-
    wọn fún Òjó.   ly and gave them to Ojo.)

Most (but not all) sentences with topical qualifiers in the language have corresponding sentences without such qualifiers. Thus, the one corresponding to the long sentence above is:

Bàbá ra bàtà ní Èkó. Ó   (Father bought shoes in Lagos.
    sáré wá 'lé. Ó kó wọn   He rushed home. He gave
    fún Òjó.   them to Ojo.)

COMPREHENSION

1. What is the normal position of occurrence of the following in Yoruba sentences:
   Predicator, Subject, Object and Pre-Verbal Adverbs?
2. What do qualifiers occur with, and where do they occur relative to what they qualify?
3. Where do sententials occur in Yoruba sentences?
4. What does the term *Basic Word Order* mean? What is the opposite of the term?
5. Name four constructions which display non-basic word order.
6. How is non-basic word order produced?
7. What is the basis for the claim that verbs play a central role in Yoruba sentences?
8. What are the distinguishing structural characteristics of imperative sentences? What are such sentences used for?
9. What are sentences with unspecified verbs? Under what circumstances are such sentences used?
10. What is the difference between splitting verb sentences and serial verbal sentences?
11. What are the differences and the similarities between serial verbal sentences, splitting verb sentences, and echoing verb sentences?

12. What are cognate nouns, and what are sentences with cognate object nouns?
13. What is the difference between sentences with cognate objects and those with cognate adverbials?
14. What are the various ways of indicating negation in Yoruba sentences?
15. What are the two types of conditional sentences in the language, and how are they differentiated?

EXERCISES

A Complete the following, e.g.

Ó jí ẹran jẹ.   =   Ó jí ẹran; ó jẹ ẹran.

a   Ó ń ṣẹ́ 'gi tà.   =
b   Ó gbé e rù.   =
c   Mú un wá.   =
d   Ó ti sá lọ.   =
e   Ó lé wọn jáde.   =
f   Igi ya dí ọ̀nà.   =
g   O tì í ṣubú.   =
h   Ó lù ú bo ilẹ̀.   =
i   Ó gbé ọbẹ̀ ka iná.   =
j   Ó ro 'nú p'ìwà dà.   =

B Complete the following, e.g.

Ó ṣòro 'óṣe.   =
{
  Ó ṣòro 'íṣe.
  Ó ṣòro ṣíṣe.
  Ó ṣòro ní 'íṣe.
  Ó ṣòro ní ṣíṣe.
  Ó ṣòro ní àtiṣe.

a   Ó dùn 'únwò.   =
b   Kò fẹ́'ṣẹ́ 'ẹ́ṣe.   =
c   Ó wá 'ákí mi.   =
d   Ó sú mi 'íṣe.   =
e   A ò mọ̀ ọ́n 'íkọ.   =
f   Yé 'épa ariwo.   =
g   Ìwé wù mí 'íkà.   =
h   Ó bẹ̀rẹ̀ sí mi 'íbú.   =
i   Ng ò níí pẹ́ 'ẹ́dé.   =
j   Kò ṣe 'ẹ́ṣe.   =

C Complete the following, e.g.

> Ó jí mi ní owó.   = Ó jí owó mi.
> Ó dá mi ní ẹ̀bi.   = Ó dá ẹ̀bi fún mi.

a Ó gbá mi ní etí.   =
b Ó pe dúdú ní funfun.   =
c Ó jà mí ní iyàn.   =
d Ó kọ́ mi ní ìwé.   =
e Ó ta mi ní ìpá.   =
f Ó pè mí ní orúkọ.   =
g Ó kún mi ní inú.   =
h Ó ń wá mi ní ìjà.   =
i Wọn ta á ní ọfà.   =
j Ó ń mọ́ mi ní ojú.   =

D Complete by inserting *pé*, or *kí*, or *pékí* as appropriate, e.g.

> Mo gbọ́   — ó wá. = Mo gbọ́ pé ó wá.

a Mo gbà   — o lọ.
b Ọba ní   — o tètè padà.
c Wọ́n ti kéde   — ẹnikẹ́ni kò gbọ́dọ̀ jáde l'ọ́la.
d Mo rántí   — o sọ bẹ́ẹ̀.
e Jẹ́   — ng tètè lọ.
f Mo fẹ́   — o wá rí mi.
g Ng ò mọ̀   — o ò níí wá rárá.
h Ta l'ó sọ   — wọ́n sùn sí 'bẹ̀?
i Ó ń ha 'lẹ̀ mọ́ mi   — òun lè nà mí.
j Mo dá a l'ámọ̀ràn   — gbogbo wa lọ.

E Complete the following, e.g.

> Ó dára pé o tètè lọ.   = Pé o tètè lọ dára.

a Kò bọ́ sí i pé o ò lọ.   =
b Ó dùn mi púpọ̀ pé o ò wá.   =
c Ó yà mí l'ẹ́nu pé wọn ò   =
   tí ì dé.   =
d Ó ṣe 'ẹ́ṣe kí wọ́n tètè padà.   =
e Ó wù mí kí ó jókòó tì mí.   =
f Ó burú púpọ̀ pé o ò kí i.   =
g Ó ti 'ni l'ojú púpọ̀ pé o
   gbẹ̀hìn.   =

h Ó sàn pékí o máà/má lọ rárá.　　=

i Ó rú mi l'ójú bí o ò ṣe bá a
　　ní'bẹ̀.　　=

j Ó dá mi l'ójú pé kò sí ní'bẹ̀.　　=

F Complete the following without referring back to the chapter on Verbs, e.g.

Ẹ̀rù bà mí.　　=　　Mo ba ẹ̀rù.

a Ojú tì mí.　　=

b Ìṣẹ́ ń ṣẹ́ wọn.　　=

c Ìyà ń jẹ wọ́n.　　=

d Àyà ń já mi.　　=

e Inú bí mi.　　=

f Ojú ń kán mi.　　=

g Wèrè ń ṣe ẹ́ ni?　　=

h Ojú ń pọ́n wọn.　　=

i Owó kò sí ní ọwọ́ mi.　　=

j Ó ta òṣì.　　=

G Employ the following verbs in sentences with cognate objects, e.g.

lọ　:　Ó lọ lílọ kan tí kò ti rò tẹ́lẹ̀.

dùn	(be sweet)	dára	(be good)
dé	(arrive)	wà	(to exist)
wá	(come)	gùn	(be long)
rù	(be lean)	bọ̀	(be coming)
pupa	(be red)	le	(be hard)

135

CHAPTER 9

Sounds

SOUNDS AND WORDS

9.1 Sentences were said in Chapter 1 to be made up of syntactic classes of words. We should now add that words for their part are made up of sounds.

SOUNDS AND LETTERS

9.2 Sounds as used here are not equivalent to letters of the alphabet. The latter are conventional symbols, in the sense that people use them by agreement or convention. People use them specifically to represent sounds on paper, wood, blackboard, etc. For this reason, they are also said to be graphic or written symbols. As such, they are seen with the eyes and sometimes even felt with the fingers. Sounds, on the other hand, are not normally seen with the eyes; rather they are heard with the ears.

SPEECH ORGANS

9.3 Speech sounds in particular are made in the mouth, nose and throat. They are made with the help of several parts and organs of the body including: Lungs, Windpipe, Vocal Cords, Nasal Passage, Oral Cavity, Tongue, Palate, Teeth and Lips.

9.4 The sounds of Yoruba are produced mostly with air forced out of the lungs. Such air passes through the windpipe and sets the vocal cords vibrating. This vibration is magnified and modified in the mouth and/or nose, and it finally reaches the outside as speech sound.

SOUND QUALITY

9.5 The nature or quality of the particular speech sound that reaches the outside depends, however, upon several things. In particular, it depends upon the role played by some of the organs of the body listed above.

The tongue can be moved about very easily. It can be moved backwards or forwards in the mouth. It can be raised or lowered. It can even be made to touch some other parts of the mouth, e.g. the one immediately behind the upper teeth, and the palate.

The lips can be firmly pressed together or be opened. They can be made to form either a round shape or one that is not round. Finally, the upper teeth can be made to rest on the lower lip.

The nasal passage can be closed or opened from the inside. The mechanism for closing and opening the nasal passage is not as subject to conscious control or manipulation as, say, the tongue.

The vocal cords are two folds of flesh inside the top part of the windpipe. When brought together, they close the windpipe completely, and air can therefore neither enter nor leave the lungs. When pulled away from each other, the windpipe becomes open, and air can freely enter or leave the lungs. The two vocal cords can also be stretched in varying degrees, that is, from very slightly to considerably. The behaviour of the vocal cords cannot be controlled at will in exactly the way that that of the tongue or the lips can.

9.6 The nature of any given sound in Yoruba (and in other languages, too) depends upon a combination of some of the events just described. Thus, the Yoruba sound represented by the letter *b* is produced with:

(*i*) the nasal passage closed from the inside;
(*ii*) air from the lungs coming out through the mouth only;
(*iii*) the tongue lying flat and inactive;
(*iv*) the lips at first firmly pressed together and then suddenly opened or released;
(*v*) the vocal cords vibrating.

All these events occur more or less simultaneously, rather than one after the other, except in *(iv)*.

CLASSIFICATION

9.7 Yoruba sounds can be divided into three kinds. They are consonantal sounds or consonants, vowel sounds or vowels, and tonal sounds or tones.

TONES

9.8 There are three main tones in Yoruba. These are called low tone, mid tone and high tone. They are represented graphically as follows:

Low tone   \
Mid tone   –   (or nothing)
High tone   /

9.9 Tones are produced with the vocal cords only. The particular tone produced by the vocal cords depends upon how much these cords were stretched. The tighter they are stretched, the higher the tones they produce. Thus, they are stretched the most tightly for high tone and the least tightly for low tone. For mid tone, they are only averagely stretched.

9.10 Tones by themselves do not carry meanings, except under special circumstances. Thus, among manner nouns, high tone tends to indicate small size, and low tone big size. For example:

bínńtín	dùgbẹ̀dùgbẹ̀	rébété	kìrìbìtì
ṣóńṣó	kìtàkìtà	kẹ́tẹ́kẹ́tẹ́	kẹ̀tẹ̀kẹ̀tẹ̀
kólíẹ́	ràbàtà	gírígírí	gìrìgìrì
róbótó	rògbòdò		

High tone, mid tone, low tone and mid tone occurring in that order tend to suggest disorder or disorganisation. For example:

ségesège	pátipàti	yánnayànna	kátakàta
játijàti	jágbajàgba	ránunrànun	pálapàla

Except in the case of the manner nouns exemplified here, the normal function of tone in Yoruba is to help to differentiate between words and even sentences. Thus, in speech the following two sentences are differentiated by tone only:

> Mo fò díẹ̀. (I jumped a little.)
>
> Mo fo díẹ̀. (I skipped a few.)

Members of the following sets of words are differentiated by tone only:

bá	(overtake, accompany)	lé	(be surplus)
ba	(hide oneself)	le	(be hard, difficult)
bà	(touch down, alight upon)	lè	(be able to)
ṣẹ́	(to break—long and thin objects)		
ṣẹ	(to come to pass)	kọ́	(to learn, to teach)
ṣẹ̀	(to happen, to offend)		

VOWELS

9.11 When vowels are produced, air from the lungs passes out very freely through the mouth alone, or through both the mouth and the nose.

9.12 Oral Vowels

Vowels which are produced when air passes out through the mouth only are said to be oral. There are seven such vowels in the language. They are conventionally represented by the letters: *i e ẹ a ọ o u.*

9.13 Nasal Vowels

Vowels produced with air passing out through *both* the mouth and the nose are said to be nasal. There are five such vowels in the language. Except in one case, they are conventionally represented by two letters—a vowel letter followed by the letter *n*: *in ẹn an/ọn un a* (as in *màlúù* (cow), *márùún* (five)).

The nasal vowel written as *an* is normally pronounced as *ọn* by most people. This is why they are listed here as alternatives.

9.14 Back Vowels

When some vowels in the language are pronounced, the lips form a round shape, and the tongue is bunched back in the mouth. Such vowels are said to be back vowels. They are:

u   un

o   —

ọ   ọn/an

9.15 Front Vowels

When some other vowels in the language are pronounced, the lips do not form a round shape, and the tongue is mostly in the front part of the mouth. For this latter reason, such vowels are called front vowels. They are:

in   i

—   e

ẹn   ẹ

9.16 Central Vowels

There are only two such vowels in the language. When they are made, the tongue is neither in the front nor in the back of the mouth. The lips are also not made to form a round shape. The vowels are:

a   (as in *ata*)

a   (as in *màlúù*)

9.17 Vowel Height

When vowels are produced, the tongue is not only moved forwards and backwards, it is also raised. At the same time, the mouth is opened, in some cases widely, and in others not so widely. The raising of the tongue and the opening of the mouth go together. The mouth is opened widest when the tongue is lowest in height, and opened the least when the tongue is at its highest level. Depending upon the vowel, the tongue can be made to assume four different heights or levels. If 1 represents the lowest level, and 4 the highest, the respective levels of the vowels in the language can be shown as follows:

High	Level 4	in	i	u	un	High
Mid	Level 3	—	e	o	—	Higher Mid
	Level 2	ẹn	ẹ	ọ	ọn/an	Lower Mid
Low	Level 1		a, a			Low

There are no nasal vowels at Level 3; hence the dashes put there.

9.18 The vocal cords vibrate when vowels are being produced.

9.19 Vowels sometimes bear meanings, as in the following cases:

a	(we)	palaba	vs.	pẹlẹbẹ
o	(you)	(flat)		(flat)
ẹ	(you (*pl.*))			
i	(him, it, her)			

However, this is not their main function. Their main function, like that of tones, is to help to form and differentiate between words. The following words are differentiated by their vowels only:

kí	(to greet)	kọ́	(to teach)
ké	(to shout, cry)	kó	(to gather)
kẹ́	(to pet)	kú	(to die)
ká	(to roll up, to pluck)		

CONSONANTS

9.20 Air coming from the lungs is generally not allowed to pass out freely when consonants are produced.

9.21 Stops
For some consonants, air from the lungs is completely stopped from going out, though only for a very brief moment. Such consonants are referred to as stops. In Yoruba, they are the consonants written as follows: *b, d, j, g, gb, t, k* and *p*.

9.22 Fricatives
Air from the lungs passes out rather noisily when some other consonants are being made. Such consonants are referred to as fricatives. The Yoruba fricatives are: *f, s, ṣ* and *h*.

9.23 For the remaining consonants in the language, air from the lungs passes out not too freely, but without making noise. These consonants are: *m, n, l, r, w* and *y*.

9.24 Air from the lungs passes out through the mouth for all the consonants in the language, except two. For those two, air passes out through the nose instead of through the mouth. The two consonants are: *m, n*.

9.25 In the table given below, consonants are arranged in columns according to how they are made.

1	2	3	4	5	6
b	t	ṣ	k	p	h
m	d	j	g	gb	
f	n	y		w	
	s				
	l				
	r				

In making the consonant sounds in Column 1, either the two lips are firmly pressed together, in the case of *b* and *m*, or the lower lip is pressed against the upper teeth, in the case of *f*. At least one lip is involved in producing each of the sounds in that column.

For making each of the sounds in Column 2, the front part of the tongue is made to touch that part of the roof of the mouth immediately behind the upper teeth.

The sounds in Column 3 are made by touching the roof of the mouth (hard palate) with the middle part of the tongue for *j* and *ʂ*, and by raising the middle part of the tongue very close to the roof of the mouth in the case of *y*.

The back of the tongue is made to touch the rear of the roof of the mouth (soft palate) in producing the sounds in Column 4.

The lips and the back of the tongue are used jointly for making the sounds in Column 5. For *p* and *gb*, both lips are pressed firmly together, and the back of the tongue is simultaneously made to touch the rear of the roof of the mouth. For *w*, the lips are made to form a round shape, and the back of the tongue is raised close to the rear of the roof of the mouth.

For the only sound in Column 6, the vocal cords are pulled far apart, and air passes out rather freely but noisily.

9.26 Consonants normally never carry any meanings. What they do is to help to form words and differentiate between them. The following words are differentiated by their consonants only.

bá	(to overtake)	ṣá	(to cut—with cutlass)
fá	(to shave off—hair)	yá	(to borrow, lend)
dá	(to break—long thin object)	ká	(to roll up)
sá	(to run)	gbá	(to sweep)
lá	(to lick)	wá	(to look for)
rá	(to disappear)	há	(to be stuck)
já	(to break—strings)	pá	(to be bald)

COMPREHENSION

1. What are words made up of?
2. What do the letters of the alphabet stand for?
3. Why are the letters of the alphabet said to be conventional symbols?
4. How do language sounds differ from the letters of the alphabet?
5. Where are language sounds made?
6. Name the organs or parts of the body involved in speech production.
7. How important is air from the lungs in the production of Yoruba speech sounds?
8. What part do the lips play in the production of Yoruba speech sounds?
9. What part does the tongue play in the production of Yoruba speech sounds?
10. Name the three major types of speech sounds in Yoruba?
11. How many tones are in Yoruba?
12. Describe the function of such tones.
13. Name the two main types of vowels in Yoruba. How many are such vowels in all?
14. What do vowels do in the language?
15. What are front vowels? How do they differ from back vowels?
16. How many vowel levels are in the language?
17. What are stop consonants? Name some such consonants in the language.
18. What are fricative consonants? Name some such consonants in the language.
19. How many consonants are there in the language?
20. What is the difference between consonants and vowels?
21. What work do consonants do in the language?

EXERCISES

A Stand before a mirror or hold one before you and watch yourself making the vowel and consonant sounds of the language. Observe the shapes of your lips and the movements (or otherwise) of your tongue as you make the various sounds concerned.

B Supply ten other examples in addition to those given in Section **9.10** of manner nouns in which high tone indicates smallness and low tone bigness.

C Supply ten other triplets in addition to those given in Section **9.10** whose members are differentiated by tone only.

D See how many sets of seven words differentiated by their vowels only you can find in the language in addition to the one given in Section **9.19**.

E Supply other examples in addition to the ones given in Section **9.26** of Yoruba words differentiated by their consonants only.

CHAPTER 10

Sounds in Combination

10.1 It is clear from earlier chapters that words are not combined just any how to form sentences. Quite the contrary, they must be combined in specific ways. What is true of words is true of sounds also: there are definite ways in which they must be combined to form genuine Yoruba words.

THE SYLLABLE

10.2 None of the three categories of sounds in the language, namely, tones, vowels and consonants, can occur by themselves, i.e. independently of the other two categories.

10.3 Tones always occur with vowels, and vice versa. For example:

Ó   (He, She, It)
Ò   (Not)

Tones can also occur with *n* and *m*,[1] as in:

Mo ń lọ.   (I am going.)
Mo ń bọ̀.   (I was/am coming.)

10.4 Consonants always occur with vowels; i.e. they never occur without accompanying vowels. The vowel that any particular consonant occurs with always follows the consonant itself. For example, in:

kí . (what?),   mo (I),   rà (to buy).

In the following example,

ilé   (house),

---

[1] These are the only two consonants on which tones can occur in the language. When these consonants occur with tones, they are to all intents and purposes the same thing as vowels; for they are then doing the work of vowels rather than of consonants. See **10.5** below.

it is the vowel *é* that goes with the consonant *l*, and not the vowel *i*.

A consonant only occurs with one vowel at a time. In other words, if two vowels follow the same consonant, only one of those vowels goes with the consonant, while the other stands independently. Thus, in:

máa

the second *a* is independent, in the sense that it does not go with any consonant.

10.5 A consonant plus the vowel accompanying it constitutes a syllable. A vowel that has no consonant attached to it also constitutes a syllable. So also do *m* and *n,* when they occur with tones. Consequently, there are two kinds of syllables in Yoruba.

  (a) syllables beginning with consonants, e.g. *rí* as in *orí* (head).
  (b) syllables not beginning with consonants, e.g. *ò* as in *Òjó; ń* as in *ń lọ.*

10.6 A word may be only one syllable long, e.g.
     Mo (I),   O (You),   rí (to see).
Or it may be several syllables long; e.g.
     agogo (bell, clock),   kòlòkòlò (fox).
These two words have three and four syllables, respectively.

10.7 Words having only one syllable each are said to be monosyllabic, those with more than one are said to be polysyllabic.

THE DISTRIBUTION OF TONES

10.8 Low tone, mid tone and high tone all occur in monosyllabic words. For example:
        bá (to overtake)
        ba (to hide   oneself)
        bà (to alight)

Low tone and mid tone can occur anywhere in any polysyllabic word—at the word's beginning, in its middle, and at its end. For example:

agogo   (bell)
agbègbè   (district)

High tone occurs anywhere in polysyllabic words beginning with consonants, but does not occur at the beginning of polysyllabic words that begin with vowels. For example:

pátákó   (plank)
akátá   (civet-cat)
ògógóró   (made-in-Nigeria dry gin)

It is because high tone does not occur at the beginning of polysyllabic words starting with vowels that the following sound strange and funny to Yoruba ears:

*ákátá   (civet-cat)
*ógógóró   (made-in-Nigeria dry gin)
*ólè   (thief)

CONSONANT-VOWEL COMBINATIONS

10.9 Not all the possible combinations of consonants and vowels are actually found in monosyllabic words. The nasal vowels in particular do not combine as freely with consonants as one would have expected. Take the case of the consonant *b* for example. The following monosyllabic words beginning with *b* occur:

bí	(if)	bẹ́	(to cut, to give way)	bá	(to overtake)
bi	(to ask)	bẹ	(to peel)	ba	(to hide one-self)
bì	(to vomit)	bẹ̀	(to beg)	bà	(to alight)
bọ́	(to drop)	bó	(to peel off)	bú	(to insult)
bọ	(to worship)	bò	(to cover)	bu	(to mildew)
bọ̀	(to come)			bù	(to break off)
				bùn	(to give as a gift)

On the other hand, the following expected monosyllabic words beginning with *b*, in fact, do not occur—as yet.

*bé	*bín	*bẹ́n	*bán	*bọ́n	*bún
*be	*bin	*bẹn	*ban	*bọn	*bun
*bè	*bìn	*bẹ̀n	*bàn	*bọ̀n	*bo

10.10 As a means of enlarging and developing the vocabulary of the language, words like these could, by general agreement, be made to express some of the useful technical and scientific concepts for which Yoruba lacks words at present. Some of the words sound very funny, to be sure. But this is largely because people are not used to hearing them. Once such words become established in the language, they will sound just as normal and acceptable as the words in the earlier list.

THE *n* AND *l* ALTERNATION

10.11 The consonants *n* and *l* are like two sides of the same coin: where you find one, you will not find the other. Thus, the consonant *l* occurs with oral vowels only as in:

bíbélì	(Bible)	lọ	(to go)
lé	(to pursue)	lò	(to use, employ)
lẹ	(be lazy)	lu	(to pierce)
là	(to split)		

The consonant *n*, on the other hand, occurs with nasal vowels only, as in:

ní	(=nín)	(to have)	nà	(=nàn)	(to flog)
nù	(=nùn)	(to wipe)			

The consonant *l* is always used instead of *n*, where the latter would otherwise occur immediately preceding an oral vowel. This is why we do not have:

*anáta	(pepper seller)	*onówó	(wealthy person)
*enépo	(oil seller)	*ọnọ́rọ̀	(affluent person)
*ẹnéja	(fish seller)		

Instead of these, what we have are:

aláta,   elépo,   ẹléja,   olówó   and   ọlọ́rọ̀.

149

The word *oníṣu* (yam seller) is all right, because the vowel that *n* occurs with there is nasal, not oral. The vowel actually ought to have been written as *ín;* for it sounds exactly like the vowel in *rín* (to laugh).

VOWEL AND CONSONANT HARMONY

10.12 Vowels co-occur with themselves in particular ways in polysyllabic nouns. This is true, more specifically, of polysyllabic nouns which begin with vowels, and have not been derived from other words.

10.13 In such words, if the first vowel is *o*, the second cannot be *ọ* or *ẹ*; and if the first vowel is *ọ*, the second similarly cannot be *o* or *e*, and vice versa. This is why we do not have:

*òlẹ	(lazy person)	*kòlọ̀kòlọ̀	(fox)
*ọlè	(thief)	*ẹjò	(snake)
*ọ̀gógóró	(made-in-Nigeria dry gin)	*ẹ̀tè	(lips)

What we have instead are:

ọlẹ	ọ̀gógóró	ejò
olè	kòlọ̀kòlọ̀	ètè

This pattern of vowel co-occurrence shows that vowels of Levels 2 and 3 cannot be mixed in the first two syllables of polysyllabic nouns beginning with vowels.

10.14 Front and back vowels, too, tend not to be mixed in the last two syllables of polysyllabic nouns. In other words, there is a tendency for front vowels to co-occur in the last two syllables of polysyllabic nouns to the exclusion of back vowels; and vice versa. This is apparently why we do not have:

*agídó	(bluff)
*òkétọ́	(bush rat)
*ọ̀gẹ̀dù	(banana)

What we have instead are:

agídí
òkété
ọ̀gẹ̀dẹ̀

This apparently is also why we do not have:

      *kòkòrì   (insect, germ)
      *gúgúré   (pop-corn)
      *orúkẹ   (name)

but, instead, have:

      kòkòrò
      gúgúrú
      orúkọ

10.15 As pointed out earlier, a consonant never occurs in the language without being followed directly by a vowel.[1] Because of this, two consonants never follow each other in the language (*gb* is a single consonant represented by two graphic symbols). Also because of this, Yoruba words never end with consonants.

Foreign words borrowed into the language are normally not permitted to break these two rules. Foreign words in which two consonants follow each other usually have the vowel *i* or *u* inserted between those consonants when the words themselves are pronounced by Yoruba people.

If the first of the two consonants involved is *b* or *p,* the vowel inserted normally is *u.* If it is any other consonant, the vowel will be *i.* For example:

búlọọkù	((cement) blocks)	síléètì	(slate)
búrẹdì	(bread)	dírẹbà	(driver)
búlúù	(blue)	gírámà	(grammar)
kíláàsì	(class)	tábìlì	(table)

The vowel *i* or *u* is attached to the end of foreign words which would otherwise end with consonants when pronounced in Yoruba. Normally, the vowel *u* is attached to *p, b,* and *m,* while *i* is attached to other consonants. For example:

bọ́nbù	(bomb)	ṣẹ́ẹtì	(shirt)
ṣọ́ọ̀bù	(shop)	bẹ́ẹdì	(bed)
sáàmù	(psalm)	féèlì	(fail)

---

[1]Notice in this connection, the *n* in *rín* does not count as a consonant. It is never actually pronounced. It merely serves to show that the preceding vowel is a nasal vowel.

Exceptions to these two rules of pronouncing foreign words in Yoruba are due to the tendency described earlier for front and back vowels to exclude each other in the last two syllables of polysyllabic nouns. This is why we have, e.g.

bíríkì	(brick)	kóòtù	(coat)
góòlù	(gold)	búlọ́ọ̀kù	(block)

instead of:

*búríkì	*kóòtì
*góòlì	*búlọ́ọ̀kì

NASAL VOWELS AND THE VOWEL *u*

10.16 No words begin with either the vowel *u* or nasal vowels in the language. Words beginning with *u* are now found in dialects only, as in the following words from the Ekiti dialects:

uṣu	(iṣu)	(yams)			
ukú	(ikú)	(death)	ùrù	(ìrù)	(tail)
uṣẹ́	(iṣẹ́)	(work)	ùyà	(ìyà)	(suffering)

CONTRACTION

10.17 Contraction is the shortening of words and phrases. Such shortening is brought about by dropping some sounds from the words and phrases concerned. Most of the cases of contraction in the standard language today involve tones and vowels. In other words, consonants are rarely dropped these days (except in such dialects as the one spoken in Ọyọ).

There are two kinds of contraction. One is a reflection of change in the language, and the other an indicator of style of speaking.

10.18 The contraction which reflects change in the language affects both vowels and consonants. As a result of contraction, the vowel *i*, with mid tone, is fast disappearing from the beginning of polysyllabic nouns. Such nouns that used to begin with this vowel no longer do so for some people today. For example:

Yétúndé	(= Iyé tún dé)	(Yetunde)	(personal name)
yàrá	(= iyàrá)	(room)	

bùsùn (=ibùsùn= ibi ùsùn) (bed)
lèkùn (=ìlèkùn) (door)
bùsò (=ibùsò= ibi ùsò) (mile)

Many nouns have been or can be contracted by having
one of their consonants dropped. For example:

àárò (=òwúrò) (morning)
ààtàn (=àtìtàn, àkìtàn) (refuse dump)
ààké (=àkíké) (an axe)
eegun (=egungun) (bone)
eégún (=egúngún) (masquerader)
oówo (=oríwo?) (a boil)
èèmò (=èmìmò) (something unusual)
aago (=agogo) (bell)

10.19 The contraction which indicates style of speaking
involves tones and vowels mostly, as said earlier. It occurs at
the boundary between two words, when the last vowel of
one word is brought in contact with the vowel at the beginning
of the word that immediately follows. The words involved
may be two nouns, or, in the more usual case, a conjunction,
a verb or a preposition followed by a noun.

10.20 Tones, as said earlier, never occur by themselves;
they always occur on vowels. Nevertheless, it is convenient to
describe the behaviour of tones under contraction separately
from that of vowels. For the behaviour of tones under contraction is completely regular, while that of vowels is not.

The behaviour of tones can be easily summarised by the
following formulas in which **H** means High Tone, **M** Mid
Tone, **L** Low Tone, + boundary between two words, and
⟶ 'becomes':

	:ewé ọbè	⟶ ewébè	(vegetables for stew)
1. H + M ⟶ H	:dé ilé	⟶ délé	(get home)
2. H + L ⟶ HL	: dá àrà	⟶ dárà	(perform wonders)
3. M + M ⟶ M	: ra ilé	⟶ ralé	(buy a house)
4. M + L ⟶ L	: ra àgbò	⟶ ràgbò	(buy a ram)
5. L + L ⟶ L	: rìn ìhòhò	⟶ rìnhòhò	(walk nude)

153

These formulas, with the exception of the second one, accurately describe the speech of all speakers of the standard language. For some speakers, the vowel bearing the low tone in Formula 2 is shortened considerably. Even so, the low tone itself is never completely lost.

10.21 The behaviour of vowels under contraction is, as already indicated, irregular. But perhaps a more accurate way to characterise it is to say that it is not easy to describe. No simple and general formulas have yet been found to describe it both accurately and exhaustively. A few examples of vowel contraction are:

ra epo →	repo	(buy oil)
lá epo →	lápo	(lick oil)
rí eja →	réja	(see fish)
ní ọjà →	lójà	(at the market)
ewé oko →	ewéko	(weeds, grass)
tẹ́ ewé →	tẹ́wé	(spread leaves)
ìdí ọkọ̀ →	ìdíkọ̀	(motor park, bus-stop)
àti Òjó →	àtÒjó	(and Ojo)

ASSIMILATION

10.22 It is not very usual to contract two nouns that follow each other. What happens instead most of the time is that the vowel of one of the two nouns changes its form or sound quality and becomes identical with the vowel of the other noun. This type of change is referred to as assimilation.

10.23 The Vowel _i_
The vowel _i_ always changes its form, no matter whether it occurs at the end of the first noun or at the beginning of the second. For example:

ilé ìwé →	ilé èwé	(school)
orí Òjó →	oró Òjó	(Ojo's head)

10.24 If the second noun in each of the above two examples began with a consonant, a vowel having a mid tone would be heard between it and the first noun. That vowel would have the same sound quality as the last vowel of the first noun. For example:

Ìwé Dàda ⟶ Ìwé e Dàda   (Dada's book)

Examples like this should be considered to be of the same kind as the examples given above. This would mean that all Yoruba nouns which appear to begin with consonants actually begin with what might be called a 'silent *i*'.[1] And it is this silent *i* which changes its sound quality, as the non-silent *i* always does, thereby yielding the kind of phrase exemplified above.

Some words were mentioned earlier under contraction which have lost their initial vowel *i* (with mid tone) in the speech of some people. This is probably the way other nouns which today begin with consonants lost their initial vowel *i*, too. However, as phrases like the one above also show, these nouns have not lost that initial vowel completely. They seem to retain it in the construction exemplified by the above example.

10.25 Other Vowels

In all other cases of assimilation, it is the vowel of the first noun which changes its sound quality. For example:

ilé Òjó	⟶ iló Òjó	(Ojo's house)
ilé Ọ̀la	⟶ iló Ọ̀la	(Ọla's house)
ilé Ayọ̀	⟶ ilá Ayọ̀	(Ayọ's house)
ilé Ẹ̀bùn	⟶ ilẹ́ Ẹ̀bùn	(Ẹbun's house)
ara Òjó	⟶ aro Òjó	(Ojo's body)
ara Ọ̀la	⟶ arọ Ọ̀la	(Ọla's body)
ara Ẹ̀bùn	⟶ arẹ Ẹ̀bùn	(Ẹbun's body)
ara Èjìdé	⟶ are Èjìdé	(Ejide's body)

TONE CHANGE

10.26 Tone change involves replacing the original tone or tones of a word by another or other slightly or vastly different tone or tones.

---

[1] In some of the existing dialects of the language, this 'silent *i*' would actually be pronounced. Thus, *Dàda* in the standard language would be *Idàda* in such dialects.

Tone change should not be confused with tonal transfer. What happens in the case of the following phrase is tonal transfer, not tone change:

jí ewé ——▶ jéwé   (steal leaves)

Following contraction, the tone formerly on *i* is transferred to the initial vowel of the noun *ewé* (leaves).

Tonal transfer occurs with contraction. Tone change on the other hand has nothing at all to do with contraction.

10.27 The most well-known of the tone changes in the language involves monosyllabic verbs. If such verbs have a low tone, when pronounced in isolation, that low tone must be changed to mid tone when an object noun not in the polymorphic noun class immediately follows. For example:

Mo mọ̀.	(I know.)
Mo mọ ibẹ̀.	(I know the place.)
Mo gbà.	(I agree.)
Mo gba ìmọ̀ràn náà.	(I accepted the suggestion.)

10.28 Other equally important but less well-known tone changes also occur in the language. One of them involves nouns whose last or only two syllables have low tone. The last low tone in such nouns becomes mid tone when the noun itself is followed by a genitival qualifier whose first tone is mid. For example:

ẹ̀wù Ayọ̀	——▶ ẹ̀wu Ayọ̀	(Ayọ's shirt)
bàtà Ayọ̀	——▶ bàta Ayọ̀	(Ayọ's shoes)
gèlè Yétúndé[1]	——▶ gèle Yétúndé	(Yetunde's head-dress)
alùpùpù Bọ́lá[1]	——▶ alùpùpu Bọ́lá	(Bọla's motor cycle)

10.29 If the last word in any sentence containing the pre-verbal adverb *mà* (indeed) has a low tone, that low tone is changed into a tone very similar to mid tone. For example:

---

[1]Notice how *Yétúndé* and *Bọ́lá* behave here like nouns (genitival qualifiers) that begin with a vowel having a mid tone. Their behaviour here further strengthens the suggestion made above that nouns that appear to begin with consonants actually begin with a 'silent' vowel, and that, therefore, all Yoruba nouns begin with vowels.

Kò mà rà → Kò mà ra.   (In fact, he didn't buy any.)
Kò mà ra fìlà → Kò mà ra fila.   (In fact, he didn't buy caps.)

10.30 The final low tone in a sentence can be changed into a tone very similar to mid tone. Sentences in which such a tone change has occurred are used to express annoyance or impatience. Thus, compare these two sentences:

Dàda dà?   (Where is Dada?)
Dàda da?   (For goodness' sake, where is Dada now?)

Compare the following also:

Ó mọ̀.   (He knows.)
Ó mọ.   (Yes, indeed; he knows.)

COMPREHENSION

1. What do tones always occur with?
2. What consonants can function as vowels? How does one know that they are functioning as vowels?
3. What do consonants always occur with?
4. When a vowel goes with a consonant, where does it occur relative to that consonant, before or after it?
5. What constitute syllables in Yoruba?
6. What are monosyllabic and polysyllabic words?
7. Where can the high tone not occur in Yoruba words?
8. Do all the possible combinations of consonants and vowels actually occur in monosyllabic words?
9. Why are *l* and *n* said to be like two sides of the same coin?
10. Why is there no word like **ẹjò* in Yoruba?
11. Why does **ọ̀gẹ̀dù* sound funny?
12. Do two consonants ever occur side by side in Yoruba? If not, why not?
13. Do words ever end in consonants in Yoruba? If not, why not?
14. Why does the English word 'block' have to be pronounced *búlọ́ọ̀kù* in Yoruba?
15. Why does the English word 'class' have to be pronounced *kíláàsì* and not **kíláàsù* in Yoruba?
16. What vowels do not occur at the beginning of words in standard Yoruba?

157

17. Are there any vowels which cannot occur at the beginning of words in standard Yoruba but which can in dialects of the language? Are the nasal vowels among them?
18. What is contraction, and what kinds of sounds does it affect?
19. What is assimilation, and what kinds of sounds does it affect?
20. How does tone change differ from tonal transfer? Give some examples of tone change in the language.
21. What purposes do such changes serve?

EXERCISES

A Determine the connection between assimilation on the one hand, and the orthographic representation of words like *iyín* (you (pl.) object), *imi* (my), *iwa* (our), and the claim that all Yoruba nouns begin with vowels, on the other.

B How would the following English words be pronounced in Yoruba, especially by speakers with no knowledge at all of spoken English?

oil, fat, spoke (noun), carpet, tile, asbestos, carbon, jet, wrong and tape.

C Draw up, exactly as in Section **10.9,** two lists of occurring and non-occurring monosyllabic words involving each of the consonants in the language other than *b*. Which consonant has the longest list of actual words beginning with it?

D Do the same thing for polysyllabic words.

E With a few minor exceptions, speakers of the language are very consistent in the way they contract vowels. This suggests that there are regular rules which speakers follow in speaking the language. Attempt to formulate such rules.

F Draw up a list of those few cases where speakers do differ in the way they contract vowels. For your guidance, one such case is:

pa 'rọ́   vs.   p' urọ́   (to tell lies)